Y0-BDU-660

Architecture 2000

9.52

Charles Jencks

Architecture 2000

predictions and methods

PRAEGER PUBLISHERS
New York · Washington

For Ruth and Gardner Jencks

N A
680
. J45
1971 b

Series editor: Mary Kling

BOOKS THAT MATTER
Published in the United States of America in 1971
by Praeger Publishers, Inc.
111 Fourth Avenue, New York, N.Y. 10003
Second Printing 1973

All rights reserved

No part of this publication may be reproduced, stored in a
retrieval system or transmitted in any form or by any means,
electronic, mechanical, photocopying, recording or otherwise,
without the prior permission of the Publisher

First published in Great Britain in 1971 by Studio Vista
Blue Star House, Highgate Hill, London N19

Library of Congress Catalog Card Number: 76-128597

Printed in Great Britain

Contents

ALMA COLLEGE
MONTEITH LIBRARY
ALMA, MICHIGAN

Time present and time past
Are both perhaps present in time future,
And time future contained in time past.
T. S. Eliot 'Burnt Norton'

It seems to me neither more nor less con-
ceivable that the future, *which is not yet*,
should influence the present than the past,
which is no more, should do so.
Gabriel Tarde *Fragment d'Histoire Future*
1896.

The mental process of foresight is one of the
essential bases of civilization. It is both the
source and the means of all undertakings,
whether they be large or small; it is also the
assumed basis of politics.
Paul Valery *Oeuvres* Paris 1957, 1025

Foreword

To give a series of specific predictions for the future, cut away from their context and ideology, is next to useless. This is why in this book on architecture, I have felt it necessary to start off with very broad issues such as general methods of forecasting, the ideologies that tend to go with them and their relevance to politics, the consumer society and revolution – because all these large forces provide the context for specific architectural prediction. After discussing these rather voluminous issues, I move on to a more detailed consideration of the way that they might be taken up by the six major architectural traditions; this comprises the main body of the book and the place where more detailed predictions are made. For instance, the influence of major biological inventions in the 1980s and '90s is predicted to result in the most significant architectural movement of this century – the Biomorphic School. Thus another reason for concentrating on broad issues is that they are often taken up as a metaphor and catalyst for architectural creation – all of which leads me back, in the last chapter of the book, to a discussion of the largest question of all: the basic shifts in belief and attitude which are now, already, underway.

Charles Jencks
London, June 1969

(1) **Nicolas Schöffer** *Le Centre de Loisirs Sexuels:* the kind of one-dimensional sex satirized by Huxley and Marcuse is now seriously suggested by an architect as a desirable, future possibility.

1 Philosophies of the future

Unavoidable futurism

Anticipating the future is as unavoidable and commonplace as breathing. Perhaps, like breathing it is also involuntary and mechanical. When we follow the flight of a bird we anticipate its future course and position; we reach out to catch a falling object; we pull back to avoid an impending blow. We are so totally implicated in guessing future events that a fundamental recognition of this fact can be found in the most abstract model of perception – the model which contends that all perception is made up of a continual interplay between two terms: hypothesis and correction, or expectation and confirmation. Even as we read the lines written on this page, we cannot help but project forward certain hypotheses as to what will come next – both on the highest level of general meaning and the lowest, visceral level of syntax and rhythm.

Given this inevitability of anticipation we might well ask why the practice of futurism currently meets with such scepticism and hostility. Perhaps it is because we do not possess a live tradition capable of projecting strong, emotional demands on the future and therefore the possible, alternative choices are not accentuated. Or perhaps it is because we are burdened with a false futurism that has succeeded all too well (1, 2, 3) – a tradition which denies the richness of life, which suppresses dissent and complexity, which trivializes sex and which offers future utopias without the slightest suspicion that they are, in fact, far worse than the conditions they are meant to supplant. An age whose futurism has produced such *different* results as B. F. Skinner's *Walden Two*, Kubitschek's Brasilia and Hitler's Third Reich can be forgiven for taking a dim view of predictions. They usually set back the clock, rather than give birth to a new, desirable form of the future. And yet even because of these dystopian failures, we should make more definite claims on events which are to come, since they will turn out to be most influenced by those who make the strongest demands.

Futura abhorret vacuum; the future is offended by not being pursued; to be alive is to be a futurist of one sort or another, because life necessarily entails expectation, projection, desire of things to come and memory. The last necessity, memory, is the irreducible truth from which the conservative starts to make his claims on the future. He argues that only from memory of the past can the future have any meaning, either as progress or change, because the meaning consists in an opposition between past and future.

Even the revolutionist agrees on this point, for revolution (in the political sense first meaning return to a better past) entails a constant dialectic between at least two terms where both are known and kept in view. However, the conservative and revolutionist differ over the very real choice of *which* traditions to keep constant and which to jettison. The conservative would argue that only by keeping the existing structure constant can we have any freedom in the future. For instance, our freedom to communicate,

(2) **Lúcio Costa** and **Oscar Niemeyer** *Brasilia* 1956–60: another example of unifying visual and social forces into one, total, overpowering direction which allows no dissent, ambiguity or memory. B.F. Skinner, the behaviourist psychologist, describes his kind of Utopia in *Walden Two*, p. 196: 'Race, family, ancestor-worship – these are the handmaidens of history and we should have learned to be aware of them by now. What we give our young people in *Walden Two* is a grasp of the current forces which a culture must deal with. None of your myths, none of your heroes – no history, no destiny – simply the Now! The present is the thing. Its the only thing we can deal with, anyway.'

Without memory, history and context, however, there is no consciousness, value or even experience – a bizarre kind of Utopia.

The two semi-spherical dishes are congresses, the twin tower is the secretariat.

travel and plan is very much dependent on such banal claims on the future as the fixed train schedules and conventional calender. Without the agreed conventions as to how many minutes there are in a day, everybody's future plans would be drastically and in our

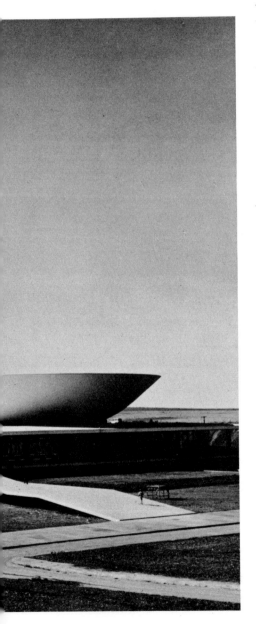

civilization, disastrously, curtailed – a point well understood by the revolutionist who attacks these pragmatic freedoms first.

Consider, for instance, the claims on the future introduced by the convention of the Year 2000. Firstly, it is dependent on the tradition of using the conventional birth-date of Jesus as a starting point, even when many have long since given up any pretensions of belief in Christ or Christianity. Although one does not anticipate the end of the world, the apocalypse which was predicted for the Year 1000, nor the outburst of Church building to celebrate the fact that this apocalypse did not occur, still one does imagine that the Year 2000 will be unusual simply because of the speculation it has generated. Ever since at least 1790, when the countdown started, there has been speculation.[1] It reached one high point in the 1890s after the publication of Edward Bellamy's *Looking Backward, 2000–1887* and quite recently has again reached flood proportions with another series of books, and even commissions, intent on marking the development towards the millennial year. The motive of number mysticism in this is, of course, minor. The books and commissions are not created *because* of the millennial number or the fact that there are three, neat zeroes; they would exist in any case. But we can be sure that the year will be quite different from any other precisely because so much effort has gone into the planning for it to arrive.

The Oedipus effect

The Year 2000 will be celebrated because we have reached it intact, or semi-intact. It will also be noted for the series of retrospective and prospective studies made to determine the accuracy and *influence of prediction*. It will be shown in countless ways that what Karl Popper termed the 'Oedipus effect'[2] has in fact taken its toll and that precisely because we predicted something (the population explosion?) it did not come about and other unforeseen consequences did:

'The idea that a prediction may have influence

1 The speculation no doubt started before this, but the earliest book on the subject I have been able to find is 'L' An Deux-Mille', by Restif de la Bretonne, 1790

2 Karl Popper *The Poverty of Historicism* Routledge and Kegan Paul, London, 1957, p. 13

(3) **Oscar Niemeyer** *The Presidential Palace* Brasilia: a classical building whose over-simplification and gross detailing betray its subsequent political usage.

1 Herman Kahn and Anthony J. Wiener *Year 2000* Macmillan & Co., London, 1967

upon the predicted event is a very old one. Oedipus, in the legend, killed his father whom he had never seen before; and this was the direct result of the prophecy which had caused his father to abandon him. This is why I suggest the name '*Oedipus effect*' for the influence of the prediction upon the predicted event . . . whether this influence tends to bring about the predicted event, or whether it tends to prevent it.'

In fact, the influence of the Oedipus effect on the population explosion has itself already been predicted. According to Herman Kahn the straight-line predictions which forecast a world population of 7.2 billion will probably have the effect of introducing preventive actions which will bring it down to 6.4 billion.[1] This example of the Oedipus effect thus illustrates two of the most important aspects of prediction: (1) there is an irreducible element of uncertainty in all social predictions caused by an unavoidable interction between observer and observed and 2) the effect of ideas and predictions on the actual course of events is, in so far as we have any freedom to direct our destiny, the essential key.

It is this last fact which makes the effect of erroneous ideas such a powerful, social disaster; in particular, any psychological idea believed strongly enough will tend to bring about a self-confirming state of affairs. Thus all ideologies, including that of the 'value-free' scientist, are radically circular and self-perpetuating. The behaviourist achieves results that show that action is pre-determined and conditioned, the pragmatist perpetuates actions that are self-serving and expedient, the social Darwinist sets off chains of events that are based on the 'struggle for existence', and so on. The problem is not that any of these ideologies are wrong, but rather that their *partial* truth can be so easily made to work as if it were *entirely* right. Given this plastic state of affairs, it is essential that any forecaster should at once make clear his own assumptions and criticize other contending positions. As will emerge in the following sections my own position, in so far as I am aware of it, is based on the theory of open systems, a theory which has been developed by biologists to explain the tendency for living things to be negentropic (or increase their order). This is not, however, to say that I accept the idea that all evolution is *ipso facto* a positive and necessarily beneficial affair.

Ideas of evolutionary progress

Consider the attitude towards evolutionary progress held implicitly and almost universally in the East and West, where technology has had its impact. It is an idea which contends, as Julian Huxley puts it,[1] that there is a general tendency in the evolution of organisms toward increased *efficiency* and increased independence of, or *control* over, the environment. This idea of natural progress is naturally favoured by Marxists and biologists in Russia, who have actually worked out an 'objective . . . calculation of progress'[2] to measure this increasing energy and control. But this same idea also underlies Capitalism and architects' in the West who, along with Buckminster Fuller, find an inevitable trend of 'doing more with less', spanning larger areas with less material (4a, b), going faster with less expenditure of energy and creating more products, and hence a conservative kind of freedom with less arduous labour.

This natural trend, which is indisputable on a certain level, has supposedly caused a major shift of consciousness in our own time which separates us from the past. The architect and forecaster John McHale, who works with Fuller on prediction summarizes the shift:

'The record of technological development is one of a progressive overlay of another form of evolution on the natural genetic process. We may date this second evolutionary period, from man's first use of tools, as marking the point when he became an active agent in his own development – when his species survival was no longer dependent on natural selection. The *consciousness* of this active participation in his own development occured quite recently – in a first groping manner around the time of the Renaissance. The consciousness of his possible *control* over his own *future* development, one would place even more recently, possibly in the decade between 1940 and 1950.'[3]

The sentiments expressed here are shared by many 'expert' forecasters, particularly those who use 'scientific methods' and sit on commissions on the future, or in 'think-tanks' like Rand Corporation or the Hudson Institute where the future is, appropriately enough, 'brain-stormed'. For instance, Daniel Bell, the head of the Commission on the Year 2000, has even spoken of the attempt to shift the old, Renaissance balance between

1   Julian Huxley *Evolution in Action* Penguin Books, London, 1963, p. 119

2   V. I. Kremyanskiy 'Certain Peculiarities . . . etc.' in *Systems Thinking* ed. F. E. Emery, Penguin Books, London, 1969, p. 146

3   John McHale '2000—' *Architectural Design* February 1967, p. 85

1 Daniel Bell, in introduction to Kahn and Wiener, *op. cit.* note 2, p. xxviii

fortuna and *virtù*[1] (Fate and directed Control) in favour of the latter by an increase in consciousness of the possible futures: that is, by stressing alternative projections. On the whole, nearly all the experts believe in technical progress as well as a major shift or mutation in man's consciousness, from a past where men believed in fate to a present where men believe in conscious control.

From an historical point of view, one can see how naive and false parts of these assumptions are. First, there have been many societies, the Greek and Roman for example, which believed in consciously shaping their own destiny, as opposed to being passive victims of fate; secondly, while there may be increasing control over lower levels of action, as the evolutionists contend, there is no

(4a) **R. Buckminster Fuller** *Air-conditioned Dome* over New York: the unconscious trend towards increased efficiency made into a conscious goal.

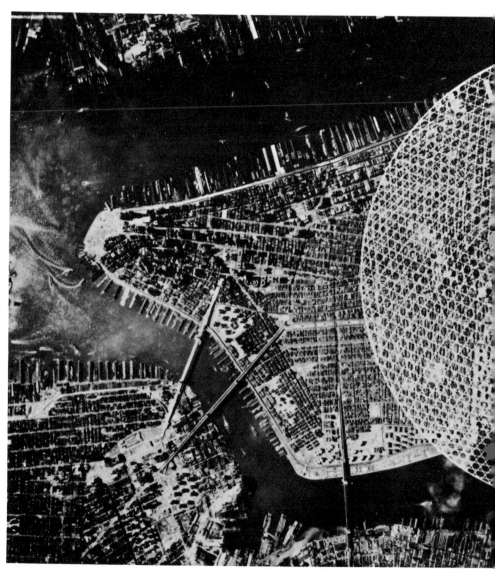

indication that the relationship between fate and control has changed on a higher level. A moment's reflection on the possible use of the hydrogen bomb should dispel any doubts about that. Yet an example chosen from their own concept of progress, such as the invention of the railroad or automobile, shows the same results. For while the automobile did represent an increase in control, speed and energy over horse-drawn vehicles, it also brought with it a decrease in control over pollution, noise and traffic jams. We may generalize from this example, which is not atypical of large scale innovations, and say that while there may be increasing control on a lower level the overall balance between control and fate remains, as the Renaissance knew, much the same on a higher level. This

(4b) **R. Buckminster Fuller** *Air-conditioned Dome* over New York: aerial perspective.

1 Bruce Mazlish *The Railroad and the Space Program, An Exploration in Historical Analogy* MIT Press, Cambridge, Mass., 1965, p. 35

is true because almost any technical innovation has both controlled, positive consequences and uncontrolled negative ones.[1] What Daniel Bell and the experts assume is that they can somehow predict some of the negative consequences (probably true) and thus shift the balance to the side of positive control. But this assumes, falsely, that one is dealing with a closed, finite system of which one knows all the parameters. In fact, as will be shown later, the distinguishing factor in

biological and cultural systems is that they are open and not closed and it is this factor, above all others, which has to be taken into account and acknowledged in any prediction because it points to the infinitude of possible consequences and their inherent dynamism, or continual self-transcendence. It is also in fact the revolutionist's answer to the conservative, or the idea of transcendental freedom as opposed to conservative freedom.

Two types of freedom

2 Known as a liberal, Galbraith's conservatism consists in arguing for a kind of technological determinism where the 'limits' mentioned are thought to be an inevitable consequence of industrialization. See his *The New Industrial State* Houghton and Mifflin, Boston, 1967, pp. 1–21, 198–209

The conservative argues that only by keeping the existing structure constant can we increase freedom through innovation and allow it to occur through choice (5). That is, only if we accept the limits of industrialization and the various forms of bureaucracy common to all industrial states, can we have the very real freedoms of communication, health and consumption which these limits bring. J. K. Galbraith, the greatest spokes-

man for this position,[2] has shown that industrialization necessarily entails a very fast changing technology and that this necessarily entails the modern, bureaucratic state composed of specialists. All this follows from an initial choice of industrialization, whether under Communism, Capitalism or any other ideology. If we want to have the freedom to travel to the moon, choose between different types of vehicle and extend

16

our lifespan indefinitely, then we have to accept specialization, bureaucracy and management of culture from above. Or do we? The revolutionist would argue that no matter which system of relations prevails at any time, we are always open to transcend it. While admitting that closed systems do tend to act deterministically so that, for instance, technology does demand specialists, it is always possible, given sufficient will and knowledge, to restructure the system. Thus it is possible, as the French 'May events' have shown, to overcome the system of relations between men that the Industrial State entails:

'You have understood nothing about our movement if you do not see this: what swept across France – to the point of creating a power vacuum – was not the spirit of professional demands, nor the wish for political change, but the desire for other relations among men. The force of this desire has shaken the edifice of exploitation, oppression and alienation; it has frightened all men, organizations, and parties directly or indirectly interested in the exercise of power, and they are attempting by all means to suppress it. They will never have done with doing so.'[1]

'*Tout est possible*, it is forbidden to forbid, the reign of imagination.' A moment in time

(5) Conservative's freedom: the freedom to choose from within a large but limited system the fruits of technical advance.

(6) Vladimir Tatlin
Monument to the Third International
Russia 1920: revolutionist's freedom, the freedom to transcend and restructure a past system. The 'moment' after revolution, before architecture solidified into the Constructivist style, and the social system solidified under the Communist party. The monument, influenced by the Eiffel Tower, consists of two interlocking helices put on an oblique angle to convey dynamism. Within these were suspended four Phileban solids to house various functions including 'political agitation'; all four were meant to revolve in accord with the cycles of the earth (year, month, day, hour), a literal form of dialectical materialism.

when all the limits of a closed system are transcended, but *only* a moment as the conservative would be quick to underline. For most people these moments of freedom only occur in single, creative acts, when any system of thought is transcended, and they exist against a vast backdrop of habitual labour. Nevertheless in all revolutions worthy of the name a brief moment is reached before betrayal, before bureaucracy sets in and before one's political destiny is handed over to a party (6). The interesting prospect of the present situation is the increasing historical consciousness which is concentrated precisely on this point.[1] Past revolutions are studied to discover the point at which the failure of nerve set in, and with it, the system of 'usual relations among men'.

Whatever one's views on this matter, one must admit that in principle the limits of any system may be transcended, whether these limits are artistic, architectural or social. This will be granted by even the most conservative realist, if only because of the great rate of change common to all fields today. Nevertheless, there is a very real and natural antagonism between the two types of freedom outlined above, an antagonism which helps explain the charges of Fascism heard from both sides when one type tends to limit the other. Yet, from an abstract point of view, in spite of their inherent conflict there is nothing really to choose between them: they are both possible and necessary. What is desired is easy to describe but difficult to achieve – the right mix.

For instance, a common prediction about the future is that the computer will bring both more control over routine bureaucracy and paperwork and more freedom to make decisions over what to do with that control. But it is also possible, not to say probable, that this increased control will be used to lessen freedom within certain systems, to increase their predictability and to determine behaviour so that it approaches certainty without limit. The modern army, the large corporation and the ubiquitous metaphor of the ant-heap or bee-hive remind us of this perpetual possibility. While this reduction of the possibilities open to man is no doubt one

(7) **Minoru Yamasaki** *World Trade Center* New York, 1969: twin 110-storey towers contain the population of a small city behind a façade that is pseudo-gothic at both ends and packing-case modern in the middle.

of the greatest and most attacked tragedies of human history, it is also one of the foundations of comedy as Bergson and the Pop artists have indicated, for it indicates a slip from the creative to the mechanical, or the perpetual nightmare of failed seriousness (7). In a gruesome sense, this is the ideal condition for the forecaster, because in such a closed system predictions nearly always come true – which raises in an acute form the question of the right combination between freedom and control, or predictability and chance.

There is a story by the poet Leopardi which illuminates part of this question of balance. It concerns a seller of almanacs, a man who sells predictions for the forthcoming year, and a passerby who is stopped on the street by the cries of prophecy.[2]

Passer-by: For how many years have you been selling almanacs?
Seller: Twenty years your Excellency . . .
Passer-by: And if you had the chance to relive exactly the life you have already had – neither more nor less, with all the pleasures and sorrows that have passed?

1 Gabriel and Daniel Cohn-Bendit *Obsolete Communism, the Left Wing Alternative* Penguin Books, London, 1969, pp. 145–204

2 Giacomo Leopardi 'Dialogo di un Venditore d'Almanacchi et di un passeggere' *Classici Italiani* Vol XVI, Milano, 1907

1 To measure progress and select evidence are two reasons usually given. See F. C. Ikle, 'Toward the Year 2000' *Daedalus* summer 1967, Boston, pp. 733–758

2 Julien Benda's *La Trahison des Clercs* 1927 is an attack on those intellectuals who, leaving their traditional role of criticizing temporal power, have succumbed to various forms of nationalism and fanaticism because of their pragmatic philosophy

Seller: No I would not wish it . . .

Passer-by: Not even *you* will turn back with this foreknowledge?

Seller: No excellency, truly I would never return.

Passer-by: What life therefore would you wish yourself?

Seller: I would wish life as it is, as God will give it to me, without other conditions.

Passer-by: Life by chance, knowing nothing in advance just as one knows nothing of the New Year?

Seller: Exactly . . .

In other words, to extract and emphasize the moral, not even the man who sells predictions could stand the boredom of having them come true in detail. Even a good year, an optimistic prediction, would be too stifling if it worked out exactly according to plan, because all the spontaneity and surprise would be gone. We would always know the outcome of every gesture no matter how wild, accidental or seemingly free. Thus we could say that what is desired of prediction is also desired of natural evolution: the humanly valuable application of chance and control, or *fortuna* and *virtù*, and not just that naturally given or existing mixture. For if it is a natural trend in technology and evolution that energy increases and efficiency becomes greater, it is also an equally inexorable trend that the rich get richer and the poor relatively poorer. It is the obligation of the predictor to augment those trends he believes to be positive and criticize those he feels negative, an obligation which he cannot altogether avoid even if he wants to. For, as already mentioned, while it is literally impossible to experience and predict without goals,[1] it is also equally true that if we do not invest the future with moral and emotional meaning, then we can neither be happy nor sad when it comes about, because we cannot even be surprised. In this sense, it is better to predict and be wrong than not to predict and remain dumb. In fact, some of the best predictions are wrong and therefore the best. For instance, George Orwell's prediction that the totalitarian state will be ubiquitous by 1984 had best be wrong, and perhaps will be, partially because he made the prediction in a form which would prevent its own occurrence. It is the least the Oedipus effect could do for us; after all we have been suffering for long enough under the false necessity of the Oedipus complex.

La trahison perpétuelle des clercs[2]

The idea that man is an unconscious victim of external forces, or internal necessities, is one of the greatest intellectual orthodoxies of our time. Ever since the waning of traditional religions, men have been convincing themselves of one inevitable necessity after another, until the point has been reached where some of them have actually started to become operative in detail. Whether or not this desire to discover some omnipotent, external force signifies an intellectual rage for order and understanding or rather a deep psychological drive to identify with a superhuman force and avoid responsibility is open to question: but its existence is beyond dispute. It can be seen in the Marxist appeal to inevitable laws of history, in the Freudian appeal to basic drives of the libido and most recently in the appeal to underlying forces of technology by Galbraith and McLuhan. It might seem at first, with such a super-abundance of prime movers, that each one would largely serve to undermine the idea that any one was primary and therefore, perhaps, the whole idea of inevitable fate itself. But quite the reverse has happened. What we have received is one fundamentalist explanation after another, with each supersession giving added hope to the belief that something really ultimate lies beneath the series of external appearances. Thus history could be seen as the gradual peeling back of layer after layer of partially true explanations which promised an absolute truth as their end. Recently, however, this search for an ultimate prime mover has reversed its direction and it now appears that if there is any such thing as an overwhelming fate it has to be considered as the concatenation of many forces together into a system, but it is even doubtful that this implies necessity.[1] For even within a rigidly deterministic system there always exists the *possibility* of transcendence and this transcendence often has an indeterminate element of chance. In any case, we have continually made the mistake of substituting a single force for the general system and having given up beliefs in a transcendental existence have located it behind and external to us. Thus Karl Marx:

'When a society has discovered the natural law that determines its own movement, even then it can neither overleap the natural phases of its evolution, nor shuffle them out of the world by a stroke of the pen. But this much it can do: it can shorten and lessen the birth pangs.'[2]

Or as a recent McLuhanism puts it:

'There is absolutely no inevitability as long as there is a willingness to contemplate what is happening.'[3]

In other words, fate is not altogether fatal as long as we are willing to go along with and understand it. A Czech proverb puts the acquiescence even better: 'When rape is inevitable, lie back and enjoy it'. In fact, this fatalism, and the examples of it that will be quoted shortly from modern architects, is merely *weak* determinism. It doesn't even have the virtue of strong determinism such as is found in the religion of Islam which argues that the inevitable is only inevitable because we cannot know it. Rather, weak determinism asserts that although we can be aware of natural laws and inevitable trends we are actually powerless to *change* them. Thus it tends to undermine our will and reconcile us to that which we *think* is beyond our power. The effects of this attitude on the future are often so unfortunate that, as Bertrand de Jouvenel says, 'it deserves to be battered in the most brutal manner'.[4] What effectively happens is that we deny that knowledge of a force allows us to do anything about it; we mistake an *inexorable* trend for an *inevitable* trend and thus implicitly mistake an 'is' for an 'ought'. Or in terms of a

1 In structuralist terms the idea of the *langue* and in systems theory the idea of the 'closed system'. See *Systems Thinking op. cit.* p. 4; Arthur Koestler *The Ghost in the Machine* Hutchinson, London, 1967, pp. 197–221. Claude Lévi-Strauss *Structural Anthropology* Basic Books, New York, 1963 argues for 'historical determinism', p. 240, but denies 'mechanical causality' p. 233

2 Preface to *Capital*; quoted from Karl Popper *The Poverty of Historicism* Routledge and Kegan Paul, London, 1957, p. 51

3 Marshall McLuhan *The Medium is the Massage* Penguin Books, London, 1967

4 Bertrand de Jouvenel *Forecasting and the Social Sciences* ed. Michael Young, Heinemann, London, 1968 p. 121 See also his *The Art of Conjecture* Basic Books, 1967, one of the best expositions of the philosophical problems underlying prediction

(8) *The Vehicle Assembly Building* Cape Kennedy: an example of 'technological determinism'. The fact that these objects transcend individual determinants and appear to be determined by many precise parameters gives them a certain moral, not to say religious, authority, especially among architects. The *VAB* 'the largest building in the world', is so large that it creates its own internal weather conditions, including an occasional thunderstorm.

former example, we assume the positive virtues of some evolutionary trend even when its correlation is that the 'rich get richer and the poor relatively poorer'.[1]

What has been the attitude of intellectuals and leading architects toward these external forces or pressures? Obviously it has been varied: both critical and passive, moral and acquiescent. Yet there is a very strong tradition in modern architecture, and one can predict its continuance into the future, of appeals to the *Zeitgeist*, or the underlying spirit of history. One might even say there has been an attempt to coerce or stampede society into accepting certain trends which the architect favours, under the guise of making them appear inevitable. I would like to substantiate this statement, but in order to avoid the misunderstanding that I am attacking particular architects or the whole modern movement, rather than an attitude of weak determinism, I will cross quote from a number of architects,[2] all of whom I agree with in other contexts.

In the early twenties Le Corbusier said: 'Industry, *overwhelming us like a flood which rolls on toward its destined ends,* has furnished us with new tools adapted to this new epoch, animated by the new spirit. *Economic law unavoidably governs* our acts and thoughts.' He was followed shortly by Mies Van der Rohe's '*The individual is losing significance; his destiny is no longer* what interests us. The decisive achievements in all fields are impersonal and their authors are for the most part unknown. *They are part of the trend* of our time toward anonymity.' Both attitudes were summarized by Nikolaus Pevsner in his justification of the modern style in 1936: 'However, the great creative brain will find its own way even in times of *overpowering collective energy,* even with the medium of this new style of the twentieth century, which, because it is a genuine style as opposed to a passing fashion, is *totalitarian.*' Although the last word was perhaps a slip of the pen and was later changed to 'universal', it is a significant slip, underlining the attitude of 'overpowering

1 For instance by the year 2000 Herman Kahn predicts that per capita income in the USA will be about $15,000 and in India $200, compared to about $4000 and $100 in 1965 (in 1965 US dollars)

2 Le Corbusier *Vers Une Architecture* Edition Cres, Paris, 1923; Mies van der Rohe *Der Quershnitt*, 1924; Nikolaus Pevsner *Pioneers of Modern Design,* 1936; Reyner Banham *Theory and Design,* 1960 (italics C. J.)

(9) *The Vehicle Assembly Building*: interior.

energy' or 'overwhelming flood' which is often connected with a particular style or technological determinism. Indeed we find a continuation of this tradition today in many places. Because of what he terms 'an *unhaltable trend* to constantly accelerating change', Reyner Banham suggests to the architect that he '*run with technology* . . . and discard his whole cultural load including the professional garments by which he is recognized as an architect' or else the 'technological culture' will 'go on without him' or Buckminster Fuller uses the example of the rigorously designed space technology (8, 9) to chide architects for not keeping up with the *Zeitgeist* and lessening the birthpangs of history. Common to all these prophecies is the appeal to a mixture of both moral choice and amoral inevitability: the conflation of an 'ought' with an 'is', or 'will be'. This position then leads to a form of pragmatism that says whatever exists, or works, is alright, or successful.

This step to pragmatism is a natural consequence of weak determinism, and its pitfalls have long been pointed out – particularly with respect to intellectuals in Julien Benda's *La Trahison des Clercs* (1927) and Noam Chomsky's *American Power and the New Mandarins* (1969). In fact the pitfalls are so well known (*Time Magazine* formulated them explicitly[1]) that only one example among many will suffice to illustrate the problem. It concerns the way in which 'the new intellectual élite', the pragmatists of the coming 'Post-Industrial Society', discuss the bombing of North Vietnam. Instead of concerning themselves with whether it is moral in principle to intervene in a foreign country and bomb, or whether these principles apply in this particular case, they are concerned with whether or not it can be successful:

'I believe we can fairly say that unless it is severely provoked or unless the war succeeds fast, a democracy cannot choose war as an instrument of policy.'

Chomsky comments:

'This is spoken in the tone of a true scientist correcting a few of the variables that entered into his computations – and, to be sure, Professor Pool is scornful of these "anti-

1 'The Tortured Role of the Intellectual in America' *Time Magazine* May 9, 1969

1 *The New York Review of Books* 2 and 16 January, 1969

2 '2000+' *Architectural Design* February 1967, p. 63

intellectuals", such as Senator Fulbright, who do not comprehend "the vital importance of applied social science for making the actions of our government in foreign areas more rational and humane than they have been". In contrast to the anti-intellectuals, the applied social scientist understands that it is perfectly proper to "rain death from the skies upon an area where there was no war", so long as we "succeed fast".[1]

The social scientists whom Chomsky is referring to are the 'New Mandarins', or the new class of intellectuals who tend to accept the assumptions and ideology of the *status quo* and then apply themselves to ameliorating its conditions. Their weak determinism consists in accepting the overall system, whatever it might be, and then applying their very real expertise to technological problems, to making the system more efficient, or humane, or smooth-running. Thus they are ready to make their peace with whatever system happens to be extant – whether it be a dictatorship, capitalism or Socialism – claiming, in Daniel Bell's famous terms, 'the end of ideology' and the fact that social problems are physical and technical rather than ideological.

The most extreme statement of this view and its consequences for the future comes from Buckminster Fuller:

'It seems perfectly clear that when there is enough to go around man will not fight anymore than he now fights for air. When man is successful in doing so much more with so much less that he can take care of everybody at a higher standard, then there will be no fundamental cause for war . . .

Within ten years it will be normal for man to be successful – just as through all history it has been the norm for more than 99 per cent to be economic and physical failures. Politics will become obsolete.'[2]

Aside from the naivety in assuming that most, if not all, wars are caused by a scarcity of material wealth, the most dubious part of Fuller's prediction consists in assuming that if man gave up his political power and turned the whole world over to administrators then all would be well. At best we would have well-fed sychophants; at worst we would live under the most successful form of Totalitarianism ever known, where no one was responsible for anything, where all tensions could be blamed on the system and where political action, or shaping collective destiny, had been perverted into occasional outbursts of violence. For, as shown in the

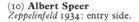

(10) **Albert Speer**
Zeppelinfeld 1934: entry side.

study of past government and revolutions, when men hand over their political powers to a party or government which is not directly responsive to their will, they give up their fundamental right to shape their destiny and alternate between passive submission and violent aggression.[1] In politics, as in an individual's way of life, there is no such thing as efficiency or specialization. To say there is would be as absurd as saying that an individual is a specialist at living.

Nonetheless, weak determinists and pragmatists assume this when they accept the present situations of politics. They assume that whoever holds political power at a given time is fated to hold it and that, in any case, the political problems will 'wither away' as the increases in production make plenty for everyone. It is therefore not surprising that the advocates of this view, let us call them 'service intellectuals', will sell their services to whoever is in power.

For instance, when the Nazis came to power in Germany in 1933, many modern architects such as Gropius, Wassili Luckhardt and Mies van der Rohe made many pragmatic attempts to achieve conciliation.[2] Gropius justified modern architecture in nationalistic terms, that is in terms of its 'Germanness'. Mies van der Rohe went so far as to sign a racist appeal from Schultze-Naumburg, an architect who was fascist enough to have dissenting artists 'bludgeoned' by stormtroopers when he gave lectures on racist art. In fact as Sibyl Moholy-Nagy has written:

'When he (Mies) accepted in July 1933, after the coming to power of Hitler, the commission for the Reichsbank he was a traitor to all of us and a traitor to everything we had fought for. He signed at that time a patriotic appeal which Schultze-Naumburg had made as Commissar to the artists, writers and architects of Germany to put their forces behind National Socialism. I would say that, of the leading group of the Bauhaus people, Mies was the only one who signed. And he accepted this commission. This was a terrible stab in the back for us.'[3]

The reasons why such incidents can occur among architects, who are otherwise rather uncompromising, remains obscure until we remember how explicitly 'apolitical' they say they are. Their disdain or hatred for politics makes them all too willing to accept the political *status quo* – if only to pretend that it really doesn't exist and has withered away. Once we have realized this fatalism as well as

1 Hannah Arendt 'Reflection on Violence' *New York Review of Books* 27 February, 1969, discusses the fact that when men hand over or lose political power they will resort to two species of violence: covert bureaucratic and overt coercion

2 B. M. Lane *Architecture and Politics in Germany 1918–45* Harvard University Press, Cambridge, Mass., 1968, p. 181

3 Sibyl Moholy-Nagy *Journal of the Society of Architectural Historians* March 1965, p. 84

(11) *Lincoln Center* New York 1961–3: drawing. The fact that neo-classicism recurs in twenty- to thirty-year cycles, is common to public building and is the result of collaborative design, makes prediction somewhat easier. Unfortunately the architects working on this project managed to produce a less successful whole together than any one of them could have produced alone – a commentary on the notorious difficulty of communal design today.

1 Philip Johnson 'Architecture in the Third Reich' *Hound and Horn* 1933

its connection to pragmatism, several other structural connections become clear.

We see how Mies's statement 'the individual is losing significance; his destiny is no longer what interests us', has parallels with Goebbels', 'It is the most essential principle of our victoriously conquering movement that the individual has been dethroned'. Or how Philip Johnson's defence of the 'new craving for monumentality' under the Nazis[1] is parallel to the 'new craving for monumentality' in the United States thirty years later (10–13). These parallels can be drawn on social, psychological and formal levels. In fact they allow us to identify structural tendencies and thus in broad outline to predict the future (the method used in pages 33–48). Thus one could point to the tendency for neo-classicism to recur, in America for instance, every twenty-five years, and its association with public building and communal design, and then predict that the next large revival will occur, significantly enough, around 1984 or so (see the self-conscious tradition). But here we come to the core of determinism and pragmatism, or the difference between an inexorable and inevitable trend.

In fact it is a characteristic of all open or biological systems to become unbalanced. This is another way of saying that in all life there is always a trend toward something or other. The systematic pessimist about the future, for example, can collect all the negative trends, which he will have little trouble finding: the population explosion, the pollution explosion and the explosive

growth of deadly weapons to take a few instances. Indeed, if things keep growing at their present rate, he can say that sometime in the twenty-first century there will not be any room to move in, everyone will be living in one, dense city, everyone will be wearing gas-masks when they leave their fallout shelters and all those people between the ages of twenty-five and thirty-four who are not bureaucrats will be scientific hippies on a jag of LSD doing Research and Develop-

(12) Architects collaborating on the *Lincoln Center* scheme, left to right: Wallace Harrison, Philip Johnson, Pietro Belluschi, Eero Saarinen, Max Abramovitz and Gordon Bunshaft.

ment for one large corporation, General, United Dynamics Inc.

All the present trends show this to be inevitable; they are all growing at exponential rates. Thus the pragmatic thing to do would be to jump on all combined bandwagons at once – a recommendation that we actually hear from some architects such as Doxiadis.[1] But, in fact, all trends do not continue indefinitely; they always reach a point of equilibrium either because counter-action is taken, because the environment is saturated or because of a counter-trend.

Counter-action depends on our knowing that a trend is inexorable, that if we do not decide to do something rather emphatic about it, it will continue into the future. Thus we may say, contrary to Marx and in accord with Islam, that the only social trends which are *inevitable* are those which we don't know

1 Doxiadis uses the metaphor of jumping on a moving train of trends, a metaphor which is fatalistic and uncritical with respect to the 'dissectibility' of forces

(13) *Lincoln Center*: the temenos.

1 The following list of
inexorable trends is divided
crudely into those we might
regard as positive and
negative; some of them are
mutually balancing.
Positive (?) exponential
growth in: scientists,
intellectuals, universities,
computers, education,
students; information,
knowledge, technology,
Research and Development
(3% of GNP), mass
research, health, recreation,
leisure; affluence, tertiary
and quarternery services;
discoveries, micro-
miniaturization, aerospace,
speed etc. Negative (?):
population, pollution,
weaponry: bureaucrats,
alienated, dispossesed,
relatively poor; over-
crowding, urbanization,
suburbanization; fashion,
pragmatists, middle-class;
centralization, loss of
privacy, spying, waste,
ugliness; small wars, change

(14) This common S-curve
or Verhulst curve shows
the usual tendency for
accelerated growth between
two levels of equilibrium.
Often exponential growth
is made up of many small
growths (small s-curves)
which escape the attention of
predictors. The large
'envelope curve' which
covers them all is thus often
too low. After *Science
Journal* October 1967.

about, and that the rest are *inexorable* and
subject to our changing them. Fortunately,
not all negative trends depend on our knowledge and desire for counter-action to disappear, but rather reach equilibrium because
of an equal and opposite trend. For instance,
the exponential growth of population, cities
and pollution might be countered by a
similar growth in contraceptive devices,
decentralization and exhaust converters. Any
sophisticated accounting of trends will show
how simple-minded it is to generate hysteria
over any single trend such as the population
explosion.[1] There are always enough balancing forces to make any particular long-term
imbalance improbable. Hence the characteristic S-curve of growth common to so many
social and natural phenomena (14). The
importance for prediction of the S-curve, or
Verhulst curve, cannot be overrated, as it
represents the most typical and basic kind of
force the forecaster tries to deal with.
Essentially it is concerned with the growth of
a force across time, or an imbalance or
pressure within an open system. Often, as in
the case of population growth, it is made up
of many smaller growth forces which are
usually misunderstood or neglected by initial
assumptions.

Thus many demographers predicted a
population limit at too low a point because
they did not assume large break-throughs in
medicine, food cultivation and transport.
Hence it is often safer to avoid specifying
exact breakthroughs in advance and draw an
hypothetical 'envelope curve' over a series of
superimposed S-curves and project this into
the future. This method is used in predicting
future transport speeds without predicting
exact methods of vehicles to attain them.

However, the concept of the S-curve is
introduced here not just to explain its general
validity for prediction, but to emphasize the
point that at any time there are always some
imbalances in a system, which are felt as
pressures. This overpowering feeling is probably as constant as the imbalances are perpetual. Since all open systems will remain
inherently dynamic and unstable, it is quite
likely that certain pragmatists and *weak
determinists* will remain ready to exploit these

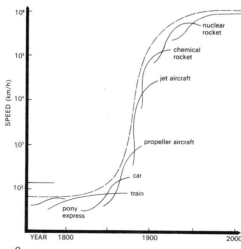

changes without regard for their moral consequences. Thus one may postulate a perpetual '*trahison des clercs*' as long as their ideology persists.

Put in an entirely different way, we could say that there will always be 'reasonable intellectuals' who regard systems as closed and deterministic, who say that given a trend X, certain consequences Y *must* follow. For instance, given our values of 'liberty and equality' in housing, it must follow that we cannot achieve 'fraternity'. The anthropologist Edmund Leach has argued that the architect's desire to create 'communities' based on kinship (or fraternity) naturally conflict with the social values of democracy, liberty and equality.[1] Thus it is eminently 'reasonable' to argue as he did, that one may have either alternative but not both. The problem with such thinking is that it does not allow for the fact that all systems can be dissected and restructured – or, in a word, transcended.

The fatalism in this case consists in regarding all systems as wholistic rather than dissectible.

1 In a lecture delivered on the future to the Architectural Association, 1 May 1969. See *New Society*, 8 May 1969

Dissectibility

Consider the tendency for all systems to form tightly interrelated wholes: in most societies, for instance, there has been a tight relationship between marriage, sexual pleasure and reproduction. In the large majority of cases, one could not have any part of the system without the whole. Now, however, because of changing values and increased technological control, it is possible to have sex without reproduction, marriage without reproduction and reproduction without sex or marriage. There are so many means at our disposal (including divorce and contraceptive devices),[2] that we can dissect the related parts of the system and have those parts we desire in any new combination we want – freed of the necessity of having them as a whole. This single example of dissectibility holds true for all wholistic systems, at least in principle. And its implications for the future are radically different from those put forward by most predictors. For it assumes that while there *is* a tendency for most systems to move inexorably in certain directions as interrelated wholes, it is always possible to dissect their positive from their negative consequences and, given sufficient effort, suppress the negative ones. To return to a former example, it was theoretically possible when the automobile came into use to foresee some of its negative consequences such as noise, congestion and pollution. If these consequences had been *predicted* and if society had been willing to pay a certain price, we would not now be confronted with more costly alternatives.

The same ambivalence of forces confronts us at every moment. For instance, there have been under development for the last ten years various forms of vehicle which move independently of any surface, route or road (15a, b). These vehicles are being developed, as Galbraith would predict, by the very largest corporations which can invest the necessary capital in specialist knowledge and production costs. Furthermore, they are being supported by the military establishment as they have very obvious consequences for use in limited guerilla warfare (16). If we apply the normal rule of thumb that 'what the few have today, the many will have tomorrow' plus a sufficient time-lag between invention and mass-production of thirty years – then we can see that by about 1990 we could have on a large scale the consequences that plague our airports even today (17). We have to dissect very consciously the obvious positive and negative consequences which these surface-free vehicles imply. On the positive side, they imply that men will be able to move over any surface they wish including ice, water and land and thus be able to cross all

2 G. R. Taylor *The Biological Time Bomb* Thames & Hudson, London, 1968. Obviously whenever we do 'dissect' wholistic systems we have to pay a very heavy price to make new combinations work satisfactorily; another biological analogy of this dissectibility is transplant surgery where the heavy price is in immuno-suppressive drugs, not to mention social tensions

(15a) *Rocket Belt* developed by Bell Aerosystems.

(15b) *Flying Bedstead* developed by Rolls Royce Inc.

boundaries, which have hitherto divided vehicles into specialized types. This will have the effect of cutting some transit times in half, removing interchange points such as ports and stations and lessening such geographic obstacles as have previously constrained location. In short the trade routes will shift, along with political boundaries which are certified by natural obstacles. For instance the political problems arising from the Suez or Panama Canal will have to move on to other constraints when hovercraft shipping becomes feasible. Cities will become more decentralized and location, due to economic factors, will take on a more even

(16) *Hovercraft* assault vehicle developed by Bell Aerosystems.

(17) *Surface-free vehicles* have the obvious consequence that men can move anywhere independent of route. This will entail legislation to control traffic and protect privacy.

"I Guess It Really Is Time To Do Something About This"

spread. As for the obvious negative consequences, they include the loss of visual and acoustic privacy, the invasion of secluded areas and the various forms of pollution with which we are already too well acquainted.

It is clear from this and other examples that to a large extent we are implicated with, and dependent on, very questionable forces and ideas. A large part of the hardware which we shall use in the future was used first in Vietnam, was developed for warfare by the largest monopolies in the world. Many of the ideas adopted here, such as the post-industrial society, come from those fatalists we have just criticized. The object of dissectibility is to take those consequences and ideas which we favour, cut away those we dislike and project forward the new combinations. This method avoids the either/or fatalism of accepting or rejecting wholistic systems the way they are presented to us. As a method, it is close to that natural evolution on which it depends; but as it demands the presence of human value and intervention, it should be distinguished from the former concept as the idea of 'critical evolution'.

2 Inexorable trends

If Trend didn't exist it would be necessary to invent Him.
After Voltaire

Question: what is the most difficult task for a Communist historian?
Answer: to predict the past.
Czech proverb

Fortune favours the prepared mind.
Louis Pasteur

As already mentioned there is no such thing as an inevitable, social trend as long as we are aware of it, because we can always, theoretically, do something about it. There are, however, many inexorable trends, trends which will continue unless we *decide* to do something rather radical about them. The importance of these cannot be overrated since, besides affecting our future lives, they underlie our assumptions and actions in a very basic way. If trends did not exist we would have to invent them, because to a large extent they constitute that common framework of continuities on which we speculate and act. With them we can construct a basic set of minimum assumptions, or what Herman Kahn calls a 'surprise-free' world – that is, a world which would come into being in complete accordance with present expectations if nothing surprising happened. Naturally nothing would in fact be more surprising than for all our detailed predictions to come true so we are caught in the ultimate paradox that the arrival of our 'surprise-free' world would be itself the greatest surprise. But this linguistic paradox need not worry us. The reason for constructing this type of framework, a projection of current trends *plus* expected break-throughs, is to create a basic model that can be used to obtain a complete picture of events that can subsequently be *distorted* as surprising things start to happen. No doubt we all carry some such model of expectations in our head anyway,[1] and the

point of constructing a standard model is to make these expectations explicit and somewhat systematic. But here an obvious question arises which can best be understood by looking at the past.

The question concerns that 'most difficult task for a Communist historian – to predict the past'. How are we to agree about large future trends when, because of the constant revision of present interpretations, we cannot even agree on what has already happened. For instance Herman Kahn has said that over the last eight hundred years a sensate trend has developed in western culture towards increasing naturalism, materialism, eroticism, professionalism etc. (18a, b, c/71) and away from the mystical, transcendental and religious outlook:

'The sensate trend goes back seven or eight centuries, but its progress has not been uninterrupted. The Reformation, the Counter-Reformation, the Puritan era in England, some aspects of the later Victorian era, and to some degree such phenomena as Stalinism, Hitlerism, and Fascism – all represented, at least at the time, currents counter to the basic trend of an increasingly sensate culture.'[2]

Even assuming this basic sensate trend to exist, it is absurd by human standards, because anyone who had lived through any of the 'counter-currents' would find such a

1 The point of the first section; see also Donald Michie, 'Machines that Play and Plan', in *Machines Like Men, Science Journal*, October 1968, pp. 86–88 and bibliography

2 Herman Kahn in *Daedalus, op. cit.*

(18a) **Kinji Fumada,
Minoru Murakami** and
Toshio Sato *Summerland*
Tokyo 1967: a fully serviced
fun palace under a space-
frame.

(18b) *Summerland :* even the
waves and ocean spray are
fully mechanized.

34

classification utterly laughable, in addition to which no one, at present, lives eight-hundred years. In short, most trends of this kind are too gross to mean anything in terms of human experience and are highly questionable with respect to their classifiers. Even supposing we could make the classifiers more delicate and appropriate, they would still never become more than an abstract, structural history, until they approached the point at which human intervention and choice became visible (i.e. the level of personal narrative). Since most prediction, including part of the present one, is structural history written forward, it will have that same gross absurdity in terms of human individuality. The only justification for this grossness is that it helps explain the common tendencies on a very abstract level.

Structural analysis

Consider the period of architectural history between 1920 and 1960 which is set out in diagrammatic form on page 40. If we had to classify it under one word we would probably use the most general and vacuous word 'modern'. Nearly everyone, even the so-called man in the street, can recognize the elements of 'modern architecture' and perhaps even surmise how it was born – from the marriage between the rational virtues of engineering (logic, function, geometry) and the visual virtues of Purism (white planes, pure forms, asymmetrical balance). Le Corbusier first made the equation around 1921, Gropius and the Bauhaus certified it by 1923 and the following years to about 1931 (known as the 'Heroic Period'[1]) saw its establishment and dissemination (19). Yet like all marriages of disparate forces it was an unstable equation that was always threatened

1 A. and P. Smithson, *Architectural Design*, December 1965. It is als called Utopian, the Inter national Style or simply Modern

35

1 Roland Barthes, *Elements of Semiology*, Jonathan Cape, London, 1967; Charles Osgood et al, *The Measurement of Meaning*, Urbana, 1957

with dissolution: from without by the growth of fascism and the resurgence of regionalism and from within by the internal inconsistency of relating abstract, pure forms to machine requirements. Thus naturally, the minute the unstable equation was made it was attacked by artists, such as Lyonel Feininger, technologists such as Buckminster Fuller, and Marxists such as Hannes Meyer.

If we consider the question of internal relations within such a period we can see that there is a *natural tendency for certain concepts and types of architecture to cluster together into a coherent whole.* This does not mean that all such clusters or traditions are monolithically consistent, but rather that they do tend to be relatively congruous. This may be partly due to the presence of similar psychological types and the coherence of developing disciplines. Thus intuitive architects tend to favour expressionist and organic forms, whereas logical designers are forced to learn a series of disciplines which are based on precision and consistent reasoning. Naturally, no particular architect can be completely classified as intuitive or logical and probably the better the architect, the less classifiable he is, such as Le Corbusier; but still, any

architect tends to favour a general cluster of concepts, to specialize in these and to distinguish himself from all the others through his specialization.

Thus without knowing much architecture, one could construct an *a priori* classification system of traditions, made up of a series of related ideas and forms and their oppositions. Such a system, called semantic space or structure,[1] would not be complete, since it is always open to new additions, but it would have the virtue of consistency. This consistency would mirror that harmony in an architect and his development. Thus we could see why, for instance, Mendelsohn's architecture was 'dynamic' because it was 'fluid' and could also be called 'expressionist', 'organic' or 'plastic' etc. (20). It is not simply that all these terms overlap or are roughly equivalent; but also that they tend to suggest development from one to the other. But what about the opposite elements in a Mendelsohn building; indeed, what about the radical shift in his work and that of all the other expressionists that occured in 1923 (21)? Consistency does not allow for this, as it does not allow for such anomalies as intuitive logic or the fluid box, nor many of the

(19) **Hannes Meyer** and **Hans Wittwer** *School* Basle 1926. Meyer later attacked the formalist part of the modern equation in his statement: 'All the objects of this world are the product of the formula function x economics. Therefore all these objects are by no means works of art.' This Marxist attack was later answered by Le Corbusier who tried throughout his life to keep the unstable equation together.

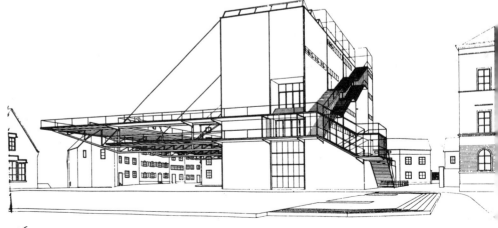

tensions which make life worth living and architecture worth inhabiting. So much the worse for consistency and structural analysis then? On the contrary, it is the existence of an harmonious model which calls attention to the value in variations, or the existence of a classification system which makes us aware that the best architects escape it. Thus, because of consistency, we are surprised, shocked and even nonplussed to find the Expressionist architects, regarded as the whole of the 'modern' movement in 1924,[1] switching, jumping even catapulting over to the International Style by 1925. What happened? There was a complete reversal of fields without a visible struggle or acknowledging statement. In fact the shift was so radical that no historian has fully come to terms with it yet, or tried to expose the problem of consistency. Consider the expressionist architecture (22) and Utopian statements of Walter Gropius in 1919:

'What is architecture? Surely the crystallized expression of man's noblest thoughts, of his ardor, his human nature, his faith, his religion. That it once was! But who of those living at this time, cursed as it is with functionalism. . . . The grey, empty, obtuse stupidities in which we live and work, will

(20) **Eric Mendelsohn** *Einstein Tower* Potsdam, 1920.

1 Architectural Review 1923–4

(21) **Eric Mendelsohn** *Villa Sternefeld* Berlin, 1923: a whole generation of architects jumped from Expressionism to Purism in three years.

(22) **Walter Gropius**
*Monument to the March
Dead* Weimar 1921: a
Utopian-Expressionist
monument to those killed
by Rightists during the
Kapp *putsch* of 1920.

2 U. Conrads and H. G.
Sperlich, *Fantastic
Architecture*, London, 1963,
p. 137

(23) **Walter Gropius**
Playboy Club London, 1966.

bear humiliating evidence to posterity of the
spiritual abyss into which our generation has
slid ... ideas perish as soon as they are
compromised ... build in fantasy without
regard for technical difficulties.'[2]

Four years later Gropius was calling for an
integration of art with technology; in 1925
he preached a kind of functionalism; in 1933
he was writing conciliatory letters to
Goebbels and in 1959 he designed eclectic
Arab architecture, The Playboy Club in
London (23) and the monolithic Pan Am
building in New York. In short, one might
say that Gropius eluded the principles of his
1919 manifesto as well as switching from
style to style. This inconsistency, which also
existed in many other architects, brings out
the problem of classification, tradition and
historical continuity in a very acute form.

For instance, since Le Corbusier was a

Utopian activist in the early twenties, should we classify him as a revolutionist or as the major figure of the Heroic Period? Is Gropius an Expressionist or Functionalist? Or the larger question that historians have yet to decide: should the whole 1919–24 period be classified as Utopian, Expressionist, Fantastic or simply Modern? These are not idle, academic questions since, apart from having political implications for future action, they go to the heart of those nexus of ideas for which an architect stands. In trying to answer them we might come to two quite different conclusions: (1) that any interesting architecture is made up of multiple classifiers and (2) that a nexus of ideas and forms continues to develop and pulsate.

Concentrating on the second conclusion, we may trace those consistent ideas and look for their common root. Thus the Utopian-revolutionist tradition obviously had a brief

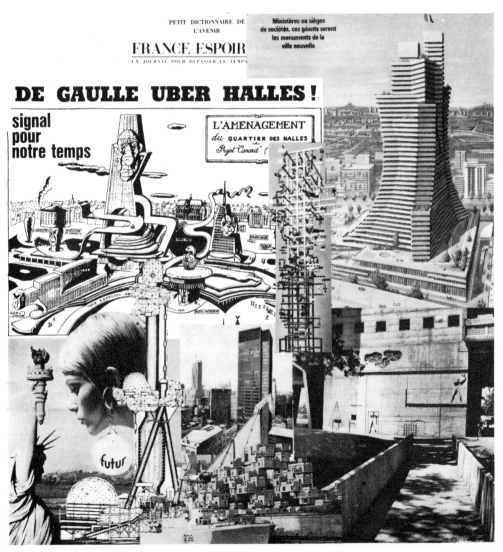

(24) **Utopie Group**
Satirical collage of futurist ideologies from Archigram and Mies van der Rohe to Le Corbusier.

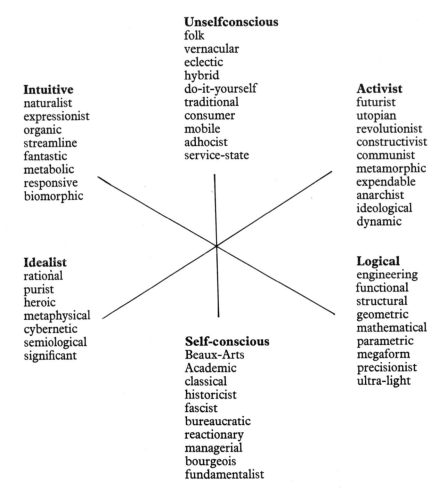

(25) *Structural diagram*
1920–2000: the six major
traditions have a tendency
to remain autonomous and
stabilize around a common
core.

Unselfconscious
folk
vernacular
eclectic
hybrid
do-it-yourself
traditional
consumer
mobile
adhocist
service-state

Intuitive
naturalist
expressionist
organic
streamline
fantastic
metabolic
responsive
biomorphic

Activist
futurist
utopian
revolutionist
constructivist
communist
metamorphic
expendable
anarchist
ideological
dynamic

Idealist
rational
purist
heroic
metaphysical
cybernetic
semiological
significant

Logical
engineering
functional
structural
geometric
mathematical
parametric
megaform
precisionist
ultra-light

Self-conscious
Beaux-Arts
Academic
classical
historicist
fascist
bureaucratic
reactionary
managerial
bourgeois
fundamentalist

1 Instead of a three-
dimensional grid a
hyperpace could be
constructed; see the
extremely interesting new
method called 'Numerical
Taxonomy', by Robert R.
Sokal, *Scientific American*,
December 1966

relationship with Expressionism and then became Constructivist and Communist until a reaction set in against it about 1931. After this it almost died, or at any rate went underground, until it surfaced again in the 1960s with the New Left, the student activists, expendable architecture, the Utopie Group (24) etc., where many of the same ideas were revived. If we analyse these ideas, as well as those of other extant movements, we will begin to see how they form self-consistent clusters that have a common core and that tend to be opposed to other clusters (25).

Such a structural analysis could be made up of many more classifiers,[1] but the six shown

here do comprehend the major tendencies which have occurred since 1920, and while further addition might increase the precision of classification it would lessen the comprehensibility. The advantage of the structural model is that it suggests as various historians such as Vasari, Wölfflin and Spengler have indicated, how civilizations tend to pulsate between opposing, polar terms. The fact that civilizations tend to go through cycles of birth, growth, maturation, death, that could be described in architectural terms as archaic, classical, baroque, mannerist, could be added to this pulsation. Thus when a cluster of concepts is explored, exhausted and used up by a series of archi-

(26) **Akin y Nozawa;** the typical megastructure envisioned by architects during the early 1960s necessitates a vast centralized state if it is to be carried through.

tects and society, either a new stage appears or a reaction to the previous cluster.[1]

But the structural model is more important for predicting small oscillations than large; and the fact that two or three traditions will oscillate in unison. Thus, whenever there is a rise in neo-fascism, there also tends to be a rise in large-scale engineering, for the obvious reason that only centralized states can carry out radical building programmes on a large scale, such as those for autobahns in Germany, large megastructures or new cities (26). Ultimately one would look for many such cross-connections between polar terms and their cyclical tendency to recur again and again in a slightly modified form. For instance, once we understand the complex nexus of ideas and forms which underlie neo-classicism, we can see not only that it tends to recur in twenty-five year cycles, but that it is preceded by certain characteristic signs which warn of its forthcoming. With such a structuralist view, it appears that nothing ever really happens in history except eternal return, 'plus ça change, plus c'est la meme chose', or what is called by anthropologists 'reversible time'.[2]

1 The concept of 'aesthetic fatigue' was first developed by Adolf Göller in 1888; see George Kubler, *The Shape of Time* Yale University Press, New Haven, 1962, pp. 81–2

2 See Claude Lévi-Strauss, *The Scope of Anthropology,* Jonathan Cape, London, 1967, p. 27

1   J. Jewkes et al. *The Sources of Invention*, MacMillan and Co., London, 1958, p. 226

2   Arthur Koestler *The Act of Creation*, Hutchinson and Co., London, 1964

3   *Ibid*, p. 194

But time is not always reversible, as the process of technological advance has illustrated. For example, the motorcycle is a direct irreversible development from the bicycle, and Einstein's conception of the cosmos rests on that of Newton.

This fact necessitates a theory of creation, a prediction about what is likely to be created, and a theory of diffusion. If one doesn't have a theory of creation, one falls into a kind of sceptical relativism upholding that all creations are unique, a matter of luck and that one cannot predict them at all:

'No one, least of all the inventors concerned, predicted the discovery of penicillin, nylon, polyethylene, the transistor, insulin, radio, the cyclotron, the zip fastener, the first aniline dye, the vulcanization of rubber or many other cases which could be quoted. More generally, in so far as specific inventions are empirical (as opposed to being constructions C.J.), they cannot be predicted.'[1]

But the authors of this long, empirical study of industrial inventions are merely being circular when they think they're being sceptical. What they are saying is that chance discoveries cannot be predicted, or that luck is merely accidental: but this is simply a definition of chance and luck and explains nothing. Fortunately we now have a very convincing model of how creation works, which can be summarized in the epigram of Louis Pasteur: 'fortune favours the prepared mind'.

As Arthur Koestler shows,[2] the creative act in all fields follows a similar conceptual pattern. First there is a preparatory period, when the mind builds up abstract models of external events, or the inventor builds up a real external model. Then either a direct discovery results – when two previously separate ideas or matrices are brought together into a new whole – or a period of tortuous search when, in some cases, the correct solution is stumbled upon *partially* by chance. The discovery of penicillin, which according to the previous, sceptical

authors was not predictable, was in fact just a typical example of this dual aspect: preparedness plus chance.

'It took more than half a century; and it was again due to an almost ludicrous series of misadventures. They started in 1922, when Alexander Fleming caught a cold. A drip from his nose fell into a dish in his laboratory at St. Mary's Hospital; the nasal slime killed off the bacilli in the culture; Fleming isolated the active agent in the mucus, which was also present in tears, and called it lysozyme. That was the first step; but lysozyme was not powerful enough as a germ killer, and another seven years had to pass until a gust of wind blew through the lab window a spore of the mould *Penicillium notatum*, which happened to settle in a culture dish of staphylococci. But Fleming had been waiting for that stroke of luck for fifteen years; and when it came he was ready for it. As Lenin has said somewhere: "If you think of Revolution, dream of Revolution, sleep with Revolution for thirty years, you are bound to achieve a Revolution one day".'[3]

Once it is accepted that the major inventions are made by 'prepared minds' doing directed research, it is a natural step to ask the 'experts' exactly what they intend to work on and when they expect to make a breakthrough. Naturally none of them can predict when or if a gust of wind, carrying their solution, will blow it through the window; but they can judge, if enough of them are deliberately working on a similar problem, when a solution is possible. Quite a sophisticated technique has been developed by the Rand Corporation for asking scientists and others what they expect to discover and when (27). The Delphi Technique amounts to a Gallup Poll of directed, 'prepared minds'. If we apply this Koestlerian model of creation to such premeditated inventions as television, the atom bomb and the moon landing, or, in architecture, the skyscraper and new city, we can come up with a simplified version of purposeful or teleological development. Let us suppose, for the sake of argument, that all developments and inventions followed this straightforward, intentional process.

First, the intention of a final goal, or the satisfaction of a felt need, would exist in the mind of an architect or designer. Then he would survey the context of possible solutions, build up various models and, with or without luck, create, invent or discover a new solution. At this point he is only at the beginning of a long process, because the solution has still to be perfected, sold to the client and then possibly taken up by others and diffused throughout a society. It has to compete with other solutions, possibly be

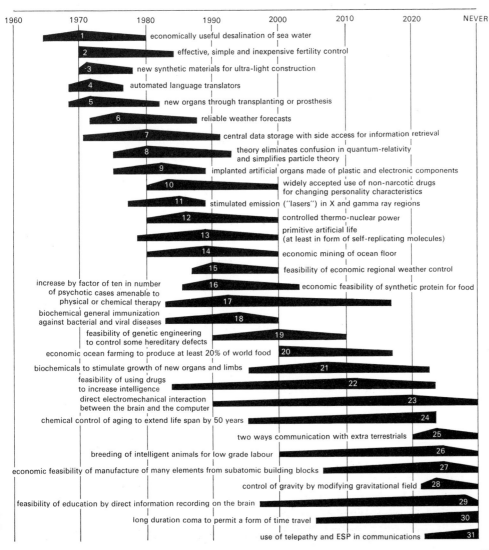

(27) *Delphi technique* predicting inventions and discoveries: the high points on the bars show the date favoured by most of the experts. After *Science Journal* October 1967.

1960 1970 1980 1990 2000 2010 2020 NEVER

1 economically useful desalination of sea water
2 effective, simple and inexpensive fertility control
3 new synthetic materials for ultra-light construction
4 automated language translators
5 new organs through transplanting or prosthesis
6 reliable weather forecasts
7 central data storage with side access for information retrieval
8 theory eliminates confusion in quantum-relativity and simplifies particle theory
9 implanted artificial organs made of plastic and electronic components
10 widely accepted use of non-narcotic drugs for changing personality characteristics
11 stimulated emission ("lasers") in X and gamma ray regions
12 controlled thermo-nuclear power
13 primitive artificial life (at least in form of self-replicating molecules)
14 economic mining of ocean floor
15 feasibility of economic regional weather control
16 increase by factor of ten in number of psychotic cases amenable to physical or chemical therapy / economic feasibility of synthetic protein for food
17 biochemical general immunization against bacterial and viral diseases
18 feasibility of genetic engineering to control some hereditary defects
19
20 economic ocean farming to produce at least 20% of world food
21 biochemicals to stimulate growth of new organs and limbs
22 feasibility of using drugs to increase intelligence
23 direct electromechanical interaction between the brain and the computer
24 chemical control of aging to extend life span by 50 years
25 two ways communication with extra terrestrials
26 breeding of intelligent animals for low grade labour
27 economic feasibility of manufacture of many elements from subatomic building blocks
28 control of gravity by modifying gravitational field
29 feasibility of education by direct information recording on the brain
30 long duration coma to permit a form of time travel
31 use of telepathy and ESP in communications

refined and perfected, and ultimately evaluated both for its good and bad consequences. We could represent this idea of purposeful development as a five-stage process (28):

(28) *Model of teleogical development.*
(over page)

1	2	3	4	5
Intention of goal	Model prepared + luck Invention	Development + sale + perfecting	Diffusion + selective pressures	Goal: good consequences kept, bad eliminated

Research and Development

Now there are examples such as the NASA Space Program or some of the work of Le Corbusier and Louis Kahn which really follow this kind of teleological or goal-directed process. Of course there are endless modifications and feedback throughout the sequence, but essentially it goes from initial goal to final result under the control and direction of the designer. Furthermore, in all cases of invention there is always a modicum of purpose and the total spectrum of inventions is neither entirely random nor unpredictable, but contains at least an element of design and preparedness.

The reason for going through this simplified explanation is to bring out the purposefulness in a process which from a sufficiently distant view, the neo-Darwinian and neo-Behaviourist position, looks random and blind. There is furthermore the present orthodoxy of chance in art (John Cage) and indeterminacy in architecture (John Weeks and others, see plates 29a, b) all of which invert this fundamental relation between chance and control.

(29a) **John Weeks** and **Llewelyn Davies** *Northwick Park Hospital* London, 1961: the first explicit indeterminate building where the structural uprights are distributed according to load and not a determined geometrical pattern.

(29b) *Northwick Park Hospital* London, 1961.

(over page)
(30) *Evolutionary tree to the year* 2000: the method for determining the six major traditions is based on a structural analysis as outlined by Claude Lévi-Strauss, without the claim to completeness which he makes. Some of the relations are obscured because the diagram is only two-dimensional, but generally speaking the pulsations represent reversible time while the inventions and movements are irreversible.

1920   1930   1940   1950

LOGICAL

INDUSTRIAL DESIGN
LE RICOLAIS TORROJA
NERVI WACHSMANN FULLER
FREYSSINET
FUNCTIONALISM   large structures
engineering HILBERSEIMER   stadia
H. MEYER
CONSTRUCTIVISM STAM
LE CORBUSIER
PURISM
DE STIJL OUD
VAN DOESBURG   **HEROIC** emigration
MIES

SAAR
SCHULTZE-
MORANDI NERV
space frame   suspensic
CANDELA   EAMES
hyperbolic-paraboloids
BRUTALISM MAEKA
geodesic **CIAM-TEAM X** SMITHSON
BAKEMA
INTERNATIONAL STYLE
LE CORBUSIER BREUEF

IDEALIST

GROPIUS TERRAGNI
BAUHAUS DUIKER AALTO
SOCIAL-IDEALIST
LURCAT

NEUTRA NIEMEYER   LC
REIDY GARDELLA
SAARINEN VILLANU

NATIONALIST
KLOTZ **AUTOBAHNEN**
SAGEBIEL KREIS G. SOTO
SPEER   monumental
NAZI
blood + soil   POLIAKOV

COSTA
neo-I
RUDOLF
UTZC

SELF-CONSCIOUS

PERRET
BEAUX-ARTS
classical

LEMARESQUIER historicist revivalist TUFAROLI
RACIST   **FASCIST** PONTI

SCHULTZE-NAUMBURG   TROOST
CAPITALIST + PIACENTINI
COMMUNIST TRADITIONAL

f
V
PI
MC
MIC
ERSKINE
SOLERI GOFF ROf
organic KIESLER BL
SCHAROUN **FAM**
HAUSE
J

BAUHAUS
expressionism
MENDELSOHN
HARING AALTO TAUT
art deco

WRIGHT
streamline   HARRIS

INTUITIVE

GAUDI
VAN DE VELDE
UTOPIAN
SCHINDLER

ACTIVIST

TATLIN VESNIN
LISSITZKY
LEONIDOV
futurism   H. MEYER
constructivism
communist

UNSELF CONSCIOUS
(80 % OF ENVIRONMENT?)

USHC   TRADITIONAL HYBRID
PRE-FAB   FHA   HOLC   USHA
GARDEN CITIES   TVA
NHA
FOLK wheatley act
VERNACULAR   barlow report   defense
REVIVAL TCPA   housing
NEP ECLECTIC   greenbelt
radburn
LOUCHEUR ACT
hauszinsteuer   **WAR MINIMAL**
NEW TOWNS
automobile radio skyscraper washing machines
tv   jets

DO-IT-Y
EAMES
HHFA   VALLINGBY FULLE
PHA   LEVITTOWN
CONS
MODE
german pr. housi
air-conditioning a
tr

1970   1980   1990   2000

MC HALE
ALEXANDER   scsd   megastructure   planet travel
                              spatial bridge tensile   INVISIBLE?
PARAMETRIC   SPACE-COLONIAL
        WOODS   MEGAFORM piezoelectric
                                                          ASTEROID TRAVEL?
                              bridge, covered cities   ultra-light
VALLE
WILSON   CUSTOM BUILT
CK   STIRLING NORBERG-SCHULZ SYSTEMS THEORY holographic design   information-rich
        METAPHYSICAL HERTZBERGER automated   laser-pipes   significant
              KALLMANN   production   explanatory   comprehensible
        urbanist CYBERNETIC   SEMIOLOGICAL
          ANDREWS   pluralist   intellectual
demic   time city
PEI   futuribles
POS   1984
GIBBERD   ROCHE   service   messianic
    YAMASAKI   bee-hive classical   reactionary
    SPENCE bourgeois   electronic highway   nature revival
                            GEM VTOL HOVERCRAFT   rocket-belt   FUNDAMENTALIST
EAUCRATIC   classical purity
CLASSICISM   PRAGMATIC   meritocratic   NEO-FASCIST
SCHOEFFER SEIFERT   POST-INDUSTRIAL   vast urban schemes
      boshwash
MEGALOPOLIS   centralized managerial
    LINCOLN-CENTER
                            vogue-affluent
                            NEW CITIES   CYBORG
                                              house robot
UTAKE BOFILL   telechiric   android   ?some major
SSELLI   fashion   invention?
    COLOMBO DOLCE VITA imagist   exoskeleton
HOLLEIN
v up   BIOLOGICAL ENGINEERING
UG-IN   plastic
IER   personalised   BIOMORPHIC
ponsive   ANARCHIST
M   workers-councils   individualist
                            hydroponic   underwater/ground
ST barriada   REVOLUTIONIST   CHEMICAL
le UTOPIE pneumatic interest community   spray-on growing structure
              advocacy   CHIMERA
STUDENT-ACTIVIST   MINORITY GROUP
DROP-CITY   BLACK RIOTS
                            geriatric
                          teeny bopper   IDEOLOGICAL
catalogue   EROTIC ANTI-FASCIST   DYNAMIC
use   HABRAKEN   LSD
ance   botch   MOOD-CONTROL ENVIRONMENTS
    GIZMOLOGY   LEISURE-VULGAR
van   GUARAN. INCOME
ard   DECENTRALIZED   WORLD-VILLAGE
        ADHOCIST   DESIGN BY
          CONTRACTUAL   COMPUTER-LIGHT PEN
          ENVIRON SERVICES SUPER SPRAWL   SERVICE-STATE ANONYMOUS
E-FAB   THIRD-WORLD GHETTO
OBILE   FREE HOUSING RENT-AN-ENVIRONMENT GUARANTEED STANDARD
EGAS   laser pipes   OF LIVING PAKS
        synthetic materials fuel cells energy packs

1 See bibliography for the eclectic list; in predicting major innovations it is better to be catholic and balanced than precise and limited

2 G. R. Taylor, *op. cit.*

3 G. Kubler, *op. cit.* discusses the history of 'objects' (art, architecture, pottery etc.) in terms of 'fibrous bundles', which are equivalent to my 'blobs'

It may be right to insist that Columbus accidentally discovered America when he was looking for India, but it is equally true that he was searching for *something*, not just sailing around in random circles. Without specifying the goals and values inherent in creation, we have no way of specifying the responsibility of an architect nor of judging whether a trend is positive or negative. Furthermore, if we consider that the sum total of development is built up of an overlay of these goal-directed processes plus the structural consistencies I have mentioned, we can project forward an evolutionary tree of the possible changes to come by the Year 2000 (30).

Several of the advantages and disadvantages of this prediction must be noted. First of all, as can be seen from the extreme left of the diagram, the six major divisions, traditions or species, are based on the six underlying structural cores. The evolutionary tree thus incorporates the tendency for traditions to pulsate, which we have already commented on; it is represented by the expansion and contraction of the blobs. Secondly, placed at right angles to this oscillating process, are the clusters of inventions predicted by experts, architects, science fiction writers and just about anyone in the prediction game.[1] These indicate the points at which major inventions are likely to be taken up by architects, affect the environment or become an inspiration for the decade. Thus if biologists predict that the decade around 1990 will see a plethora of fantastic, biological breakthroughs,[2] it is not rash to expect that 'the biological age' will have a great influence on architects, will provide them with specific tools and analogies and be taken up by the 'intuitive' tradition to become the 'Biomorphic School' of architecture. The same holds true in other key fields such as cybernetics and space research;

architects are already exploring the vast implications of both.

Thus the evolutionary tree comprehends the two kinds of time: reversible and irreversible, structural and creative, cyclical and one-way. But the diagram has very serious deficiencies which should be pointed out. Firstly it is in two-dimensions rather than three, so that all the cross relations between traditions, except those lying side-by-side, are obscured. A more truthful model of events would show many strands continually intersecting and bending through 360° as architects shifted from one tradition to another and were deflected by external influences.[3] This continual intersecting shows the major difference between 'architectural species' and 'natural species' for only the former can jump from one to another, marry whomever they please and produce offspring. It is simply that ideas and forms can cross-fertilize endlessly and capriciously, whereas, for instance, turtles do not successfully mate with giraffes.

The second principal deficiency of the evolutionary tree is that it is one set of trends projected in time rather than a series of alternatives. In the more sophisticated projections of Herman Kahn, several possible worlds are presented which rely on changes in assumption; here only one specific sequence is worked out in any depth. It is hoped that what is lost in flexibility will be gained in richness, so that the alternative sequences can be worked out by others, if they want, from the same material. In any case, the great advantage of the evolutionary tree, like that of the surprise-free projection, is that it provides a basic framework for speculation, against which variation and distortions can be seen. The sequences which follow will discuss each semi-autonomous tradition in turn, starting from the bottom of the diagram.

3 The unselfconscious tradition

(Vernacular – do-it-yourself – consumer – mobile – adhocist – service State)

Inasmuch as the unselfconscious tradition of architecture is responsible for about 90 per cent of our total environment, many architects have been consciously trying to affect it for a long time. It represents a vast area – an opportunity for some, a wasteland for others, but its hugeness consistently attracts a flood of rhetorical statistics. If it is defined in terms of that area which the architect does not *design*, it is responsible for about 98 per cent of the world; if it is defined in terms of that area which is *uninfluenced* by the architect, the figure is reduced to about 80 per cent.[1]

In fact the way it is termed and conceived is of interest in itself. Before the nineteenth century, it would have been conceived, if at all, as background – as man's biological

1 Constantinos A. Doxiadis, *Architecture in Transition*, Hutchinson, London, 1963, p. 75

(31) *Siena* illustrates the clear distinction between public and private, act and behaviour, foreground and background, common to cities before the Industrial Revolution. After this point the concept of vernacular building became conscious and sought after.

49

(32) *Las Vegas*: the electric
environment that disappears
by day.

condition from which he distinguished himself through action (31). But after this point, because of egalitarian ideas and slum conditions, it was both romanticized as 'vernacular' and debased as 'mass culture' produced by 'the masses'. In our own time, the revolutionists eye it with expectation, hoping to lead it out of exploitation; the organization men and large firms hope to sell it their services; the dictators approach it with the desire for order and control; the reformers hope to ameliorate its conditions through piecemeal legislation. Each group in turn projects its image of humanity in the abstract and then hopes to shape it. But all of these approaches ultimately prove to be in vain, because the unselfconscious tradition, like the unconscious, is continually intractable. It always outdistances directives from above; it always responds to orders in unforeseen ways. Even in such places as Russia where central control is strong, planners cannot force the people to decentralize the city and resettle according to plan. Indeed, short of wartime conditions, it appears that the environment has always acted as a self-regulating system, with the decisions coming mostly from below. One could say that it has never been more than 5 per cent controlled from above – if architects are taken to represent that control on a physical level – so that, in fact, it has never been consciously *designed*.

But this brings us to the definition of the unselfconscious tradition. Obviously, from what has already been said about teleological development, it is absurd and condescending to say that people are not conscious of shaping their own environment. In fact, if deliberate intention is taken as our criterion, then we could probably say that 100 per cent of the environment is and always has been consciously directed, because people have always taken an interest in their own particular destiny. Thus, when we use the term 'unselfconscious tradition', we will only be referring to those decisions which, while purposeful on a small scale, *are made without regard or reference to the whole* or centralized control system which exists. It follows from this definition that the key question is how much and what kind of selfconscious control

(33) **Charles Moore** and **William Turnbull** *Faculty Club* University of California 1968: neon light banners in the Great Hall.

should be exerted from above. For instance, the recent celebration of Las Vegas by architects, Tom Wolfe, and others brings up the question of whether they are equal to the task of being convincingly vulgar and exuberant, which the unselfconscious tradition is without trying (32–3). Or on another level, mass housing would probably improve in every respect if governments gave people ample funds rather than designing the housing. The same is true of welfare systems; they are much better run from below, where decisions are relevant, than from above where they tend to be costly and unresponsive.[1]

In this sense, the recent trends of 'participatory democracy', 'selectivist welfare' and anarchy are all much more efficient and beneficent than the alternatives currently practised in East and West, for they give freedom and control where it is needed.

If we return to the concept of dissectibility (p. 29), we can see why this is true. As pointed

1 Arthur Selden, 'The Welfare Crisis', *Encounter*, December 1967

1 Arthur Koestler, *The Ghost in the Machine*, Hutchinson and Co., London, 1967, pp. 45–58

2 *Ibid.*, p. 110. Koestler does not explain how precisely he asked the centipede.

3 'Adhocism on the South Bank', *Architectural Review*, July 1968.

out, any system is made up of a series of interrelated parts all of which have a certain autonomy and independence from each other. In architecture, for instance, the electrical system is independent of the heating system, the plumbing, circulation, air-conditioning, acoustical and enclosure systems (34). But it also relates to these systems and is sometimes so totally integrated with them that no repairs, or dissection, can occur without disrupting the whole. When a system has this two-way action, partial autonomy and partial dependence, Koestler calls it a 'holon'[1] because it is both a whole over a smaller part and a part of a larger whole. In more general terms, we can say that such a system, or 'holon', has internal control of its own subsets and is represented on the next higher level as an element. Thus for instance the heart beat is modified from above by the nervous system when excited, but it can also continue according to its own rhythm even when removed from the body; or the speed of a car is controlled from above by the driver, but not the order in which the cylinders fire and valves open and close. The point of these examples is that they bring out the autonomy that exists in every system, an autonomy that can be disrupted when too much control is exerted from above. Koestler gives other examples of the results of this interference such as the ossified bureaucracy or the 'paradox of the centipede':

'When the centipede was asked in which precise order he moved his hundred legs, he became paralysed and starved to death, because he had never thought of it before, and had left it to the legs to look after themselves. We would share a similar fate if asked to explain how we ride a bicycle.'[2]

Or if we tried consciously to direct the whole environment from above. The general rule to be drawn from these examples is that freedom consists in autonomous control at each level in the hierarchy, with just enough coordination with other levels to allow the whole to function. Or in environmental terms, freedom consists in the ability to modify and select those parts which are relevant to the *particular problem at hand*. For this kind of freedom, I have elsewhere coined the term 'adhocism', because it points

(34) *Home wiring kit* for owner installation: one of the many new do-it-yourself systems.

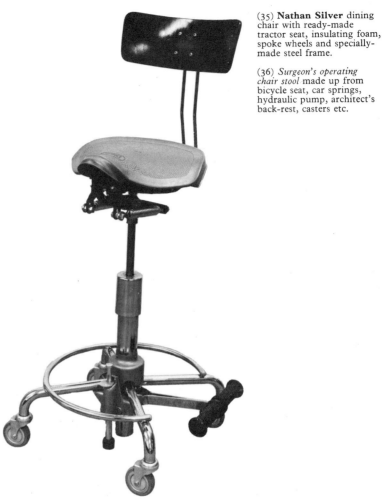

(35) **Nathan Silver** dining chair with ready-made tractor seat, insulating foam, spoke wheels and specially-made steel frame.

(36) *Surgeon's operating chair stool* made up from bicycle seat, car springs, hydraulic pump, architect's back-rest, casters etc.

to the ability to join pre-existing parts *ad hoc* – for this particular purpose.[3] A variety of examples of this can be given, from the extreme of building up new wholes from ready-made parts (36) to the more usual case of adding ready-made parts to those which are specially-made (35, 37). One of the great advantages of this approach is that it personalizes the mass-produced item by incorporating it into a whole which is built by an individual and this often throws up diverse and rich juxtapositions denied by more integrated design. Thus an accidental association with a ram's head is not to be unexpected (35). Another advantage is the considerable saving in cost and time compared with specially-made products. The individual can buy the parts he wants directly without waiting for all the intermediate stages, such as production and sales, to be completed. But in all these cases the principles remain the same: a system is dissected from a larger whole, transplanted into a new context for a particular purpose, without interference from above.

During the last twenty years a specialized industry has grown up to support this kind

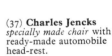

(37) **Charles Jencks** *specially made chair* with ready-made automobile head-rest.

53

(38) *Shopping by post :* the mail-order business has been in operation on a large scale since the Sears-Roebuck catalogues of the nineteenth century. As shown by this confusing layout it is still producer- rather than consumer-oriented.

SHOPPING BY POST

A message to every woman from slim and beautiful Finnish model Patti Svenson:

My figure secret...

homesauna

INFRA-RED

* SEND NO MONEY for free 14 day home trial

ONLY £39 · 19 · 0

1   See unpublished thesis of Stuart MacDonald, 'Do-it-Yourself', Architectural Association, 1969, p. 22; Building Research Station Survey, London, 1960

of autonomy. The 'do-it-yourself' industry now has more than 20,000 shops in Britain and a turnover of more than four billion dollars a year in the US. In the home a radical shift has been made from specialized to amateur labour. Such rudimentary activities as painting and wallpapering are now largely the concern of the 'homeowner', who is responsible for more than 50 per cent of domestic alterations and repairs.[1] Effectively, man is returning to his primitive state as *bricoleur* or tinkerer, aided by the large selection of consumer products with their instruction booklets and 'How-to-do-it' magazines. The specialist or middleman is effectively pre-shrunk at the factory and

54

delivered through the mail in the form of an operating manual (38) or else the product is purchased directly and explained in the supermarket-department store – shopping centre (39a, b).

Many additional aids are now being developed that should help the consumer gain more independence and control. These vary from the consumer guides such as *Which* to the computer-telexphone with light pen (40). Ultimately the individual could just sit in one place daydreaming about a project, scratching away on a television screen with a light pen, calling up product after product to see how it suits his taste, until all the ready-made resources of a society or the world were exhausted. All the technologies already exist and it is only a matter of time before they are diffused on a wide scale, perhaps even reaching the home. What would be the role

(39a) *Ikea* Sweden: the drive-in department store offers a free information service including a current catalogue.

(39b) *Roosevelt Field Shopping Centre* New York.

1 Besides Le Corbusier's early writing there is Sigfried Giedion's *Mechanisation Takes Command*, Oxford University Press 1948; Reyner Banham's 'The Great Gizmo', *Industrial Design*, September, 1965; David Greene's two articles in *Architectural Design*, July 1968, May 1969

2 *Architectural Design* July 1968, p. 314

of the architect with such decentralized design? If he interfered in this process, it would be one more paralysing question to the centipede. Rather, he would either program or design the resources, or else, more probably, stand back and select significant examples, getting excited about alternative combinations and trying to transmit this spirit of *bricolage* to others (41). So far only a few architects have been really interested in the consumer industry and discovering the poetry inherent in multiple choice.[1] David Greene of the Archigram group, has taken by far the most radical approach and shown the ultimate condition of treating all products as a type of information service:

'It's all the same. The joint between God-nodes and you, eat-nodes and you is the same. Theoretically, one node could service the lot. There's no need to move. Cool it baby! Be comfortable, Godburgers, sex-burgers, hamburgers. The node just plugged into a giant needery. You sit there and need – we do the rest! Green stamps given!'[2]

This was written by Greene after a trip to the USA, and the article, on the way consumer choice could make the environment more responsive, called attention to that large part of the environment which the architect abhors, if he ever notices it. Unfortunately there is good reason for this abhorrence, because in spite of Greene's insistence, there is as yet no consumer system delicate enough to respond to all and every individual's need and there is no likelihood that one will ever exist because of the forces of production and sales. As Galbraith and Marcuse point out, even the most plural of business firms has to spend a great deal of money in managing specific demand so that they can specialize and mass-produce a restricted range of products (5). Nevertheless within this range there does exist a relative degree of freedom, if people are willing to exploit it.

Already the five hundred largest firms in the USA have planned their range of domestic products for the next few years. These vary from ultrasonic dishwashers to thermo-electric serving carts that blow hot and cold, from luminescent walls and curtains that are sparked off by excited phosphers to remote control radios in touch with the master switch at home, so that one can turn on and off the garden spray, cook the food, clean the house, empty the garbage, wash the car (again by ultra-high frequency vibration) and

(40) *Design sketch pad* with telexphone, light pen, computer, and TV screen all hooked up to an information bureau containing the society's products.

(41) *Red Sands Fort* Thames Estuary (first noticed by Archigram): the role of the architect in the unselfconscious tradition may well be just observing and commenting on emergent possibilities and products. This one led to many later projects such as *Walking City* (pl. 80).

rotate the TV antennae while all the time one is playing bridge a hundred miles away. Perhaps only the select few will be able to live up to this high standard of culture, but for the rest there are many liberating products which the smaller firms are providing (42).

One of the most constant predictions for the near future is a shift in relation to our products from ownership to rental, from tangible possession to potential credit. Already by 1961 the credit-card world was a 60 billion dollar business in the USA alone. It could lead to the point where we could rent one piece of environment on credit, drive it where we want, take it apart when we get there, throw away half of it and trade in the other half for a new piece of environment – all without owning a thing. In fact this pattern of rental

(42) *Energy package* which supplies, in one autonomous unit, power, space heating, hot water, refrigeration, and air-conditioning. In the future such energy packs will become even smaller and further decentralize living patterns (see pl. 44). Made by Energy Conversion Ltd, England.

(43a) *Airstream caravan:* reflective aluminium bent for strength and riveted.

(43b) *Airstream caravan:* application of aircraft technology to the mobile home produces a consumer durable.

The Environment-Bubble

Transparent plastic bubble dome inflated by air-conditioning output

(44) **Reyner Banham** and **François Dallegret** in their *Un-house* 1965: the standard-of-living package plus inflatable dome push mobility and transcience towards their extreme limits.

and mobility has now reached a point in the USA where one fifth of the new homes are movable, and some so technically and visually striking that they have a high trade-in value and will never be thrown away (43a, b). However, most consumer products are meant to be dispensable and this trend has led some polemicists, notably Reyner Banham, to propose the ultimate in throwaway living where all the products including clothing are dispensed with and the artifacts – such as they are – come through the electric media incorporated under an inflatable dome (44). The two ideas behind this are to give everyone a 'standard-of-living package' containing all the necessities of modern life (shelter,

food, energy, television) and to do away with all the permanent structures of building, so that nature would remain untouched and men would not be constrained by past settlements.

The advantage of pushing present tendencies to such extremes is that the extremes indicate possibilities not otherwise exploited and present alternatives in a clear light. Perhaps the furthest limit to increasing ephemerality is either religious mysticism, or a mood-controlled environment which is induced entirely in the mind – through drugs, and electrodes implanted on the brain. In this situation all artifacts would disappear entirely

(45a) **Charles** and **Ray Eames** *Case study house* California, 1950.

(45b) *Case study house :* all the parts – industrial sash, plywood panel, metal decking etc. – are from a catalogue.

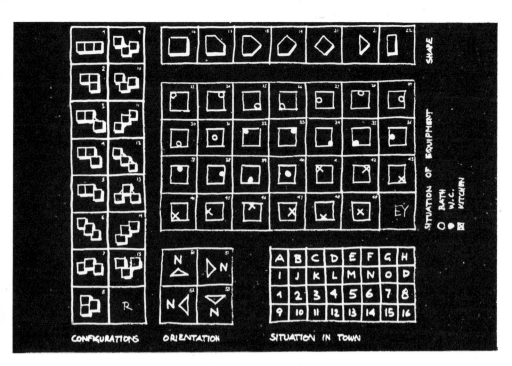

Within the image:
CONFIGURATIONS ORIENTATION SITUATION IN TOWN
SHAPE
SITUATION OF EQUIPMENT
BATH W.C. KITCHEN
KEY

(46) **Yona Friedman**
Osaka board 1970: the individual types out his specifications on a kind of typewriter with preselected alternatives and selects his ideal arrangement of rooms and location within a city (*see overpage*).

and the only thing left would be a contemplative trance having much the same advantage over tangible things that St Bernard pointed out over eight centuries ago. It may be doubted whether the mood-controlled environment was exactly what he was proffering, but there can be no doubt – what with the eight-century trend toward a sensate culture and the present possibility of stimulating the pleasure centres of the brain – that certain groups will be tempted to construct it. What exactly it would look like is best left to the imagination.

Starting from the same assumption, a consumer world, but going in the opposite direction toward structure and stability, are the projects of Charles Eames, Yona Friedman, N. J. Habraken, Martin Pawley and others. Charles Eames and his wife designed their own home in 1950 almost entirely from catalogue parts. It has that crispness and beauty, not to say stability, usually associated with custom-built designs (45a, b). More recently Yona Friedman has designed a system where the individual can type out his ideal environment and see its

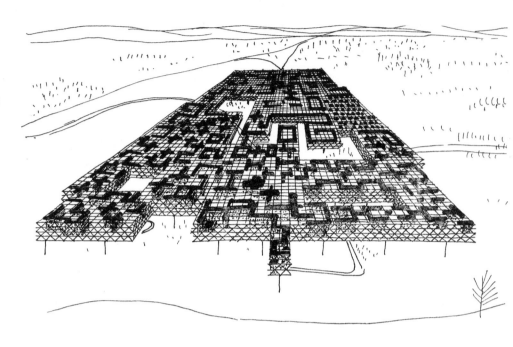

(47) **Yona Friedman**
Spatial City 1970: this three-dimensional web can undergo all possible transformations with little friction. An 'ideal infrastructure' it carries all the services and functions on a space frame supported at 200 ft intervals which, ideally, would disappear when fully clothed by a living culture.

1 Ferdinand Lundberg *The Rich and the Super-Rich* Lyle Stuart, New York, 1968. He points out that in spite of the capitalist ethic of self-betterment there is in fact very little movement between economic strata: the top 1 per cent own ⅓ of the assets and have for the last forty years

implications within a city structure (46, 47). But it may well be that the attempt to affect the unselfconscious tradition through such a system is misconceived and that the more appropriate way is to give everyone enough power and money to shape his own environment. While this might take a revolution in society, again it might not. Such proposals as a minimum guaranteed income, negative taxation and selectivist welfare are now being seriously considered in the United States and England. There is, furthermore, a general rise in affluence. While none of this would alter the inequitable distribution of income,[1] it might lead by the year 2000 to the concept of the Service State which guarantees a minimum standard of living. This would be guaranteed not by providing 'free' medical care and housing (the impossible myths of the Welfare State, all services have to be paid for by someone), but rather by restoring the free market place and giving everyone the purchasing power to select what he wants from within it. This would avoid the prob-

lem which universal welfare now brings; when the price of a commodity is depressed so that everyone can pay, the demand is forced up and the *per capita* supply is thus choked off. A Service State where a minimum income was guaranteed would not only avoid the myth that things can be free, but also avoid the usual degradation of welfare such as long waiting lists, inefficiency, means tests and arbitrary rules which break up the family and which make people conform to a system rather than be served by it. Just how the Service State will be run and to what extent it will exist in a society is obviously dependent on each country. But there is a general consensus in the East and West, among both the bureaucrats and the revolutionists, that certain economic minima should be guaranteed. Obviously these minima will not be enough, particularly in the Third World where poverty and misery will be greater than they ever have been – unless the continual protestations of the *activist tradition* are heard and acted on.

4 Scenario of the conscious traditions

Inevitably the idea of a Service State will be repugnant to many because it will seem to cut off the fundamental right of the individual to shape his political destiny and way of life. Even if all the necessities of life were guaranteed and even if there were an equitable distribution of resources, men would still be subject to social coercion, conflict, and manipulation in subtle ways. Indeed after the economic constraints have withered away because of affluence, just as many new constraints seem to be created. These could be called in the most broad terms 'cultural constraints' as they comprehend all the forms of social exchange except the merely utilitarian. Obviously these constraints, or in semiological terms, 'signs', relate to utilitarian functions but in any culture they also form their own independent system – the totality of sign behaviour. Thus when poverty for a family in Los Angeles is defined as not having two cars, a television set and telephone, part of the definition refers to the economic hardship caused by this lack of urban necessities and part refers to the conventions which are specific to what is called the 'Bar-B-Q Culture'

In every society there are endless conventions, customs and representations – in short all the sign systems – which manipulate and repress men. Thus we could say, paraphrasing Marx, 'sign-users of the world unite, throw off your chains, you have nothing to lose but your surplus repressions, clichés and manipulated needs'. The only problem with this formulation is that it does not point to the positive and inescapable use of signs. Since the West is fast approaching a condition where subsistence poverty is a minority affair and where there is an 'information explosion', or a superabundance of communicating systems, it seems natural that a tradition will evolve which can help explain the environment to men. Thus I have predicted the rise of the Semiological School in about 1990 which will grow out of the idealist tradition and see its main purpose as making the 'information rich society' comprehensible.

If one refers back to the evolutionary tree (p. 46), one can understand the logic of several other large-scale interactions which are also predicted. First of all it seems reasonable to project forward into the 1970s several strong trends of the moment. Everywhere in the world the bureaucratic and neo-Fascist tradition is explicitly under strong attack. This does not mean that this tradition is not powerful, in fact the most powerful; but rather that except in the case of a few reactionaries it works in a covert way, unwilling to admit or publicize its underlying intentions. The contrast with Fascism in the thirties should be underlined and emphasized, because Fascism was then explicitly on the march and wishing to take over. Today, however, it is publicly discredited and popularly out of fashion: very few would admit to being Fascists and all governmental coercion has to take place behind closed doors, while the pretence of democracy is maintained. The present architectural movements also reflect this anti-Fascist and pro-revolutionary mood. The two most *conscious* movements in architecture, that is the two which generate the most amount of news and are committed to influencing the whole environment from above (as opposed to the unselfconscious tradition) are the cybernetic and revolutionist. Both of these are explicitly committed to pluralism, change, individualism and minority groups – in short to fighting bureaucratic and centralizing tendencies.

It seems reasonable to assume, in spite of sporadic counter-reaction, that these two traditions will continue and become in the 1970s the two, major movements in architecture. The objective conditions for their justification will continue to exist: that is, extreme poverty in parts of the world, a suppression of minority interests and an explosion of information technologies.

5 The self-conscious tradition

(Bureaucratic – meritocratic – Post-Industrial – Neo-Fascist – vast urban schemes – revivalist)

But here, once again the paradox of consciousness must be emphasized, because underlying these explicit movements will be the unacknowledged continuation of the bureaucratic tradition which will account for the majority of building. One has only to remark on the fact that after Lincoln Centre was built in the early sixties, thousands of cultural centres sprang up across America (48) based on the same neo-classical image and the same corporate design policy; they *never achieved* great consciousness in the architectural press or innovator's mind because they were too unexceptional. One can predict the continuity of this covert existence until the point where the force of counter-reaction becomes a conscious movement. Using the European situation of the early thirties as an historical analogy, one may postulate the following kind of scenario.

Sometime in the 1980s there will be a strong,

(48) **Welton Beckett** *Los Angeles Music Center for the Performing Arts* 1965: compare with pl. 11.

1 Herman Kahn in
Daedalus, op. cit. p. 719

world-wide movement to make the pluralistic and confused situation of the sprawling cities into manageable wholes. The first voices heard are those of the academic urbanists, a group of architects who show how the overwhelming inefficiency of the cities can be stopped by rationalizing the lines of communication so that they resemble the grid patterns of the past. There is a minor classical revival which stresses the ancient virtues of harmony, purity, calm and reason. Several polemicists in the press point out, with good reason, that conflict, lawlessness, impersonality and uprootedness have gone too far (49). There is a violent attack on the vast, impersonal housing schemes in the large megalopolises such as 'Boswash'[1] (Boston-Washington city with a population of 60,000,000) or 'Parihavre' (the linear, industrial belt stretching from Paris to Le Havre and then even across Belgium deep

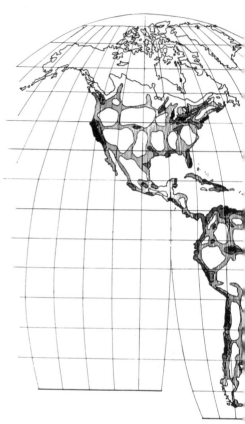

(49) *Sarcelles*: mass housing outside Paris. These developments will have become so ubiquitous by the 1980s that extremist measures will be supported on a popular scale.

into West Germany (50). It is pointed out how industrialization has destroyed feelings of place and identity, how all housing schemes 'look as if they were put together anywhere and set down anywhere by messenger and as if they could just as well be anywhere else. . . . Actually they are the work of the nomads of the metropolis, who have lost entirely the concept of homeland, and no longer have any idea of the house as inherited, as a family estate. . . . They make sleeping, eating and drinking . . . into a business, and put the whole of life on a purely materialistic basis.' Against this materialism, a new kind of housing is urged that 'gives one the feeling that it grows out of the soil, like one of its natural products, like a tree that sinks its roots deep in the interior of the soil and forms a union with it. It is this that gives us our understanding of home, of a

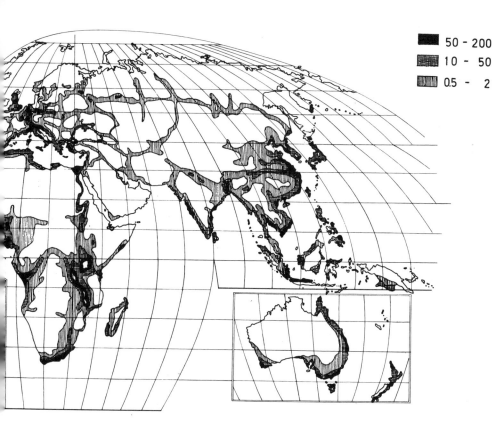

50 – 200
10 – 50
0.5 – 2

(50) **Constantinos Doxiadis** *Ecumenopolis*: an endless linear city housing thirty-five billion people is predicted for the end of the twenty-first century.

bond with blood and earth; for one kind of men this is the condition of their life and the meaning of their existence'. Except for the reference to 'blood and earth' this polemic of the Nazi architect Schultze-Naumburg[1] might have come from today's reactionary, romantic, revolutionist or avant-garde. It points to the nexus of similar ideas which we have heard since the Industrial Revolution and to the fact that they are based on objective conditions: the realities of impersonality, uprootedness, mobility and materialism which the machine has introduced into modern life.

1 B. M. Lane, *op. cit.* p. 139

(51) **Paul Maymont** *Structure for Paris* 1963: the vertical city suspended on steel cables like a bridge. Like so many megastructures projected by architects for the future, the object is formally convincing while politically questionable.

Some of the many electric cars under development

(52b) *Peel Trident*

(52a) *Quasar Khanh*

(52c) *Ford Comuta*

1 Brian Richards, *New Movement in Cities* Studio Vista, London, 1966; Gabriel Bouladon, in *Science Journal*, October 1967. Both comparative studies are excellent and show the wide variety of possible systems

The methods that the self-conscious tradition will introduce to cope with these realities will consist in such old techniques as neo-classicism and a return to 'law and order' and more sinister, new ones such as centralized data banks containing the records of each individual, wire-tapping, and as far as environment is concerned, megastructures (51) and vast urban schemes including new cities and electronic highways. One must dissect here the possible positive and negative aspects. For instance, while Hitler introduced one of the most tyrannical forms of centralized government, he also had the autobahns built and initiated the idea of a 'Volkswagen for everyone' – two projects which most people would regard as positive. It is characteristic of centralized states that they can and do carry out rather drastic, large-scale innovations: Haussmann's transformation of Paris under Napolean III is another example.

The kinds of radical transformation in urban transport which might occur under a centralized state are too numerous to list here[1] and having already mentioned 'surface-free vehicles' and caravans (17, 43), I will confine my remarks to two kinds of systems likely to develop. First electric cars (52), being developed in various forms by most of the large automobile firms in the world. The advantages of these over petrol cars resides in the absence of noise and fumes and the potential miniaturization of the engine or prime mover. Assuming a breakthrough in the technology of electric storage, one can foresee the evolution of the car towards a smaller and smaller vehicle until by the year 2000 the wheels finally disappear and the engine shrinks to a quarter of its present size, or perhaps is replaced entirely in the road itself (53). In projecting this pattern one must keep in mind what has already been said about systems and dissectibility. The sub-systems of a car – the prime mover, the wheels, the passenger and luggage space – are all fairly autonomous and evolve at different speeds. While it makes sense to assume that the prime mover and wheels will change, it is unlikely that the passenger and luggage space will alter radically. Given the vast investments

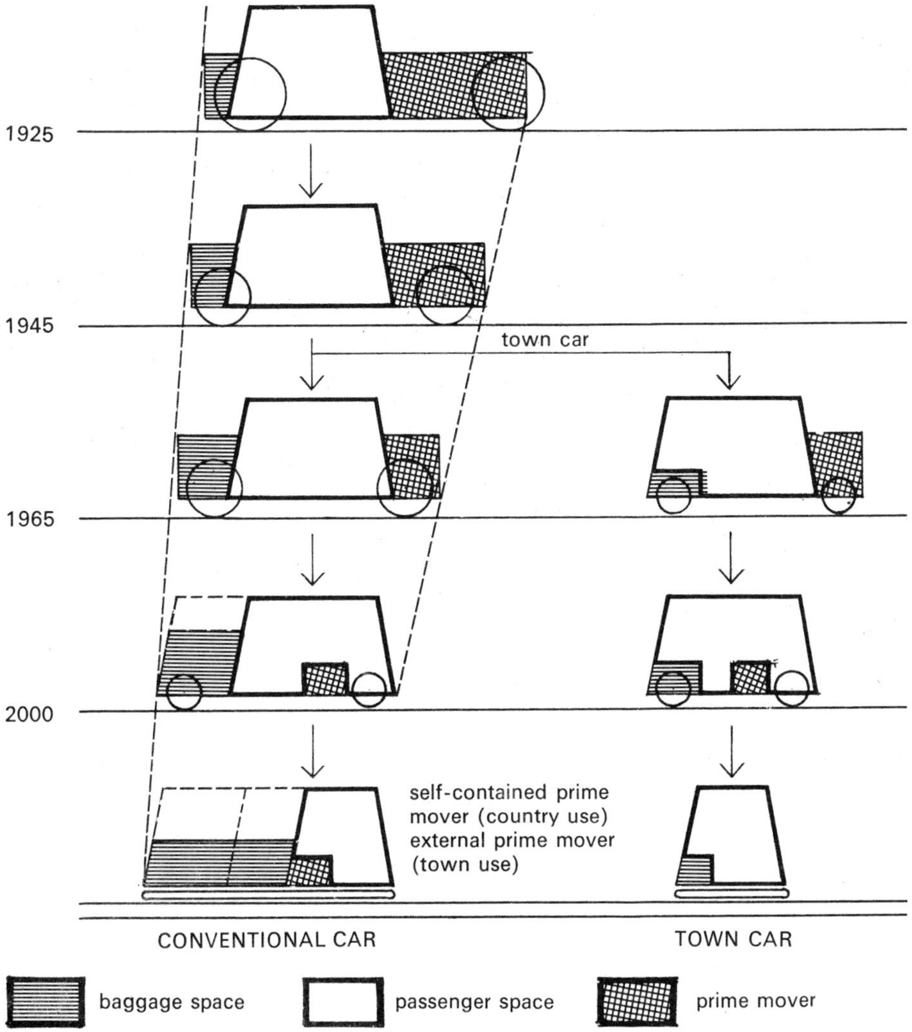

(53) **Gabriel Bouladon** *car evolution towards increasing miniaturization*: the sub-sets, or holons, remain the same except for the wheel which is replaced either by air bearings or magnetic suspension, and the engine which is incorporated in the road.

1925

1945

town car

1965

2000

self-contained prime mover (country use)
external prime mover (town use)

CONVENTIONAL CAR

TOWN CAR

baggage space　　passenger space　　prime mover

in past technologies (including roads) plus the limitation on possible combinations of sub-systems, it is possible to predict the future additions with a fair degree of accuracy. They include such sub-systems as a clip-on guide-rail which can hook on to an auto-mated highway (54) and an automatic pilot which can take over all routine driving. With such relatively cheap sub-systems, the electric car could be brought quickly into the city, easily stored in automated car parks and stripped of its more objectionable elements which are at present causing the deterioration of the 'downtown'.

(54) **Ford Motor Company** *clip-on attachment of the Mustang :* fully automated travel under computer control would keep a fast, steady flow.

(55) **Gabriel Bouladon** *continuous integrated transporter* picks up four passengers at walking speeds and accelerates them to transporter speed.

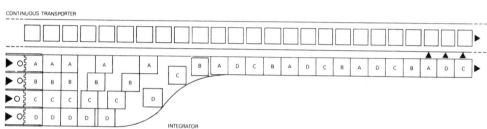

(56) **Brian Richards** and **Warren Chalk** *City interchange system* 1966: four movement systems together form a fifth which has to be worked out separately to make speed and transition an enjoyable affair.

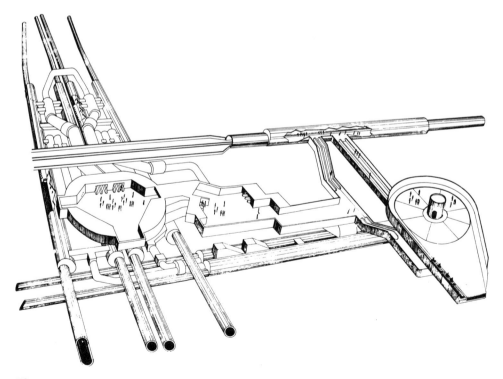

The other main system which can be envisaged for urban use will evolve from the old moving side-walk, which enjoyed great popularity at the 1900 Paris Exhibition. But it will be superior to past forms of conveyor-belt transport by being continuously moving (55) and integrated with other systems. Indeed, the main problem with all movement systems is the time wasted between interchange points, usually so great that it equals the time actually spent in moving. In order to surmount this problem, many architects are considering movement in the abstract and designing interchange systems which integrate all the various forms of movement into one, continuous flow (56). At present, the only example of such sophistication and integration exists at Disneyland (57) where the sheer enjoyment of movement is so great that many people ride the systems for their own sake without caring much for what they are supposed to be observing. But obviously the key question arising from all such transport systems and urban redesign is 'how much centralization and control do they imply?' How much personal freedom would have to be given up to achieve the political organizations which such integrated systems entail? The question is seldom posed this way, except by philosophers; and one must confine oneself to very general answers since, at present, there is no precise way of estimating relative freedoms.

Obviously, a large tyrannical state like that envisaged in George Orwell's *Nineteen eighty-four* could bring these systems into existence. It would clearly be a neo-Fascist state, entailing some quasi-religious movement that demanded extreme personal sacrifice and a return to the past and fundamentalist beliefs. But one can also predict that the far more libertarian state of the Post-industrial Society might bring them into being through piecemeal, monopolistic enterprise – in the West a far more likely alternative. Such a society would not be based on physical coercion, threats and a Police State but rather the very real pleasures which come from conforming to the large bureaucracies, the meritocracies, the 'techno-structure', the 'technetronic society'[1] and the service industries which will characterize

(57) **Disneyland** continuous *Peoplemover* with drive-wheels in the road is integrated with mono-rail, sky-ride and various other systems.

(58) **Herman Kahn** and **Anthony Wiener** fifteen criteria of the post-industrial society.

THE POST-INDUSTRIAL (OR POST-MASS CONSUMPTION) SOCIETY

1. PER CAPITA INCOME ABOUT FIFTY TIMES THE PRE-INDUSTRIAL
2. MOST "ECONOMIC" ACTIVITIES ARE TERTIARY & QUARTERNARY ("SERVICE"-ORIENTED) RATHER THAN PRIMARY OR SECONDARY (PRODUCTION-ORIENTED)
3. BUSINESS FIRMS NO LONGER THE MAJOR SOURCE OF INNOVATION
4. THERE MAY BE MORE "CONSENTIVES" (VS. "MARKETIVES")
5. EFFECTIVE FLOOR ON INCOME AND WELFARE
6. "EFFICIENCY" NO LONGER PRIMARY
7. MARKET PLAYS DIMINISHED ROLE COMPARED TO PUBLIC SECTOR AND "SOCIAL ACCOUNTS"
8. WIDESPREAD "CYBERNATION"
9. "SMALL WORLD"
10. TYPICAL "DOUBLING TIME" BETWEEN THREE & THIRTY YEARS
11. LEARNING SOCIETY
12. RAPID IMPROVEMENT IN EDUCATIONAL INSTITUTIONS AND TECHNIQUES
13. EROSION (IN MIDDLE CLASS) OF WORK-ORIENTED, ACHIEVEMENT-ORIENTED, ADVANCEMENT-ORIENTED VALUES
14. EROSION OF "NATIONAL INTEREST" VALUES?
15. SENSATE, SECULAR, HUMANIST, PERHAPS SELF-INDULGENT CRITERIA BECOME CENTRAL

1 Besides the work of Galbraith and Bell, see Z. Brzezinski, 'America in the Technetronic Age' *Encounter* January 1968 and Michael Young *The Rise of the Meritocracy* Thames & Hudson, London, 1958. The idea of a meritocratic élite of scientists and professionals leading society is an old leitmotif of science fiction going back to H. G. Wells and ultimately Plato's *Republic*

1 Cited by Daniel Bell in *Technology and Social Change,* edited by Eli Ginzburg, Columbia University Press, N.Y., 1964

2 See 'Notes on the Post-Industrial Society', *The Public Interest,* No 6 1967

the Post-industrial Society. Already in America, the meritocratic élite of highly-educated specialists has taken over from the entrepeneur in large corporations. To give one example, it appears that the Dupont Company is managed by nine men, five of whom have PhDs.[1] It would not be rash to foresee a time when all managers would have to be professors as well. As Daniel Bell makes clear in his essay on the Post-industrial Society,[2] the economic activity of the future will be tertiary and quaternary (service-oriented) rather than primary or secondary (production-oriented) (58). Thus a typical, large megalopolis will contain about 60 per cent office workers or their equivalent, who will provide each other with those specialized services such as communication, education and banking, that depend on the 'knowledge industries'. The 'organization men' of the fifties will thus give way to the 'service-intellectuals' of the

seventies – men who are trained and re-trained at university, who look on all social problems as soluble through 'social engineering'.

The first architectural project to reflect these forces was designed by the Japanese architect Kenzo Tange and his team of Metabolists in 1960. It was a plan for the Tokyo Bay Area, but was meant to be applicable to all future cities of 10 million people and more (59). The architects tried to provide a linear, open system which could accommodate the different rates of fast metabolic change common to the tertiary economy. Thus, for instance, the different traffic systems are separate from each other and grow in a series of autonomous loops – each loop being added onto the spine as it is needed. The same separation of metabolic rates can be seen in the office and residential areas (60, 61) where all the functions with the same life-span are

(59) **Kenzo Tange** and **Metabolists** *Tokyo Bay Plan* 1960: the centre of the linear spine contains roughly 60 per cent of the floor area given over to service industries such as offices and administration while the residential areas are located off the spine to each side.

grouped together. Although the Metabolists have not actually built a new city yet, they have built many fragments of their total idea and one can get a clear picture of its implications. For instance, Kenzo Tange's Yamanashi Radio Center (62) shows the usual monumental separation between elements that one has come to expect in all Metabolist building. This monumentality has been heavily criticized because, inappropriately, it is tied to the most ephemeral of functions, such as mechanical equipment. But in my view the more damaging criticism concerns the social implications of planning new cities of 10,000,000 people under the aegis of a nation-state and tertiary economy.

The first question is whether one should pile up such a density of tertiary industries in isolation from the rest of society. Apart from the fact that this would exacerbate the growing friction between the meritocratic élite

(60) *Tokyo Bay Plan*: central spine carrying tertiary industries: the office towers at the top are twenty-storey bridges spanning service pylons.

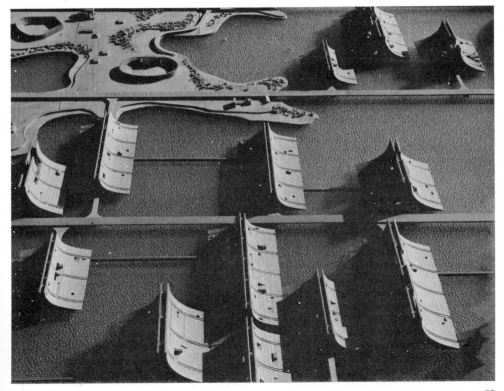

(61) *Tokyo Bay Plan*: residential megastructures with interior recreation areas, garages and schools etc.

(62) **Kenzo Tange** *The Yamanashi Press and Radio Center* Kofu 1967: this Metabolist building again shows the separation of service pylons and office buildings with empty space left for expansion.

and the rest of society, ultimately it would also be boring because of its lack of diversity. The second question concerns the political aspects of building any megastructure. In the twentieth century, the only political regimes which have been capable of such single-minded building – the kind of building most architects favour for reasons of consistency – have been highly centralized and tyrannical in one of two ways: either Fascist and coercive or bureaucratic and conformist. Assuming a surprise-free world to the year 2000, the first sort of government is unlikely to arise in the West and the latter will continue to exist and rise and fall according to the ideology of the moment. If it enjoys the kind of popularity which is here predicted for 1984, then it will be largely because the objective conditions for its existence have not been ameliorated and because the activist tradition has not formulated an acceptable alternative.

6 The activist tradition

(expendable – revolutionist – anarchist – interest group – advocacy – ideological)

The activist tradition contains the strongest critics of the present system and its apologists. Whether or not one agrees with their ideology and solutions, it has to be admitted that they are the most vociferous critics of the questionable assumptions underlying the *status quo* and ought to be considered for this reason alone. An amusing and typical example of this critical spirit can be given, it concerns the question of ideology itself. As mentioned, many advocates of the Post-industrial Society claim that most of the problems of the Industrial Revolution have already been solved and that it is just a matter of time before the rest give way to enlightened social engineering and piecemeal reform. These advocates of the present system proclaim 'the end of ideology' and announce the exhaustion, not to say corruption, of all ideology itself. Yet as shown by the New Left, Noam Chomsky and others,[1] this 'end of ideology' is itself ideological in the classic sense of the term, because it is a nexus of similar ideas and habits which justify the underlying social conditions of its upholders. Thus one has the ludicrous situation that precisely when 'the end of ideology' is being proclaimed, 'the continuity of ideology' is being assured – a paradox which has its instructive side. For as long as there is inequity, there will be ideas which support and attack it, so one may safely predict the continuity of ideology to the year 2000 and way beyond.

The activist tradition excels at exposing these paradoxes and laying bare anomalies which most people accept as a matter of course. For instance, why should governments try to do everything in their power to suppress squatter settlements when often they work so much better than the government housing that is supplied at much greater cost and effort? A most striking example of this absurdity occurred in Lima, Peru where at least one quarter of the population now live in squatter settlements, or *barriadas*. The way these *barriadas* were formed is instructive.[2]

After the Second World War, they spread very quickly because of rapid urbanization. They were immediately regarded as social evils, as seedbeds of communism and as centres of crime and prostitution. In fact, as it turned out, the realities were quite different: the incidence of crime was much lower than in the urban slum and the sociopolitical views of the inhabitants were, ironically enough, conservative. But the government, social workers and architects were determined to regard them as social evils, and therefore they were made to fit this role at all costs. Naturally, the would-be squatters became activists in a literal sense. The only way they could gain rent-free land and leave the unendurable, urban slum was to form organized platoons and *invade* government-owned land during the night (63). Invasions.

1 Besides the work of Chomsky and Cohn-Bendit already cited, see *Student Power*, ed. Cockburn and Blackburn, Penguin Books, Harmondsworth, 1969, particularly Blackburn's 'A Brief Guide to Bourgeois Ideology'

2 William Mangin, 'Squatter Settlements', *Scientific American*, October 1967; John Turner, 'The Squatter Settlement: architecture that works', *Architectural Design*, August 1968

(63) Night-time layout for a new *barriada*. The rest of the invading squatters, as many as 1000, will soon arrive in trucks and taxis.

(64) Right after the invasion when the police have been defeated the first stage of the *barriada* is set up out of sheds made of mats.

had to be carefully organized with an avant-garde made up of lawyers to choose the site, lay-out men to draw the boundaries for streets and lots, and a woman known as the 'secretary of defence' whose precise role is somewhat obscure but whom one imagines acting both as a normal secretary and a buffer to the police. After an invasion (there have been more than a hundred around Lima) the police manage to counterattack and lose (64, 65), or if they do happen to win and clear the site, it is only a matter of time before it is reoccupied and sooner or later recognized by the authorities. Then given a few years, a two-stage development sets in where the squatters set up more permanent abodes, built of cement rather than straw, and start their own form of sociopolitical organization. Soon they are organizing yearly elections of their own governors in a country where local democracy was unknown for more than sixty years. Inevitably there are drawbacks of an administrative kind: the squatters have trouble constructing large-scale facilities such as sewer systems and often have to depend on the central city for schooling. But the area in which they undeniably excel is in community spirit and popular initiative. There are endless examples of communal construction and communal services and, perhaps more important, self-help. In the *barriada*, the individual can construct and destruct his house according to need without government interference. For instance, if he needs a second story or a new room he can add one without restriction; if he needs a yard for raising chickens and guinea pigs he can chop down an old room. Thus the needs are satisfied according to individual priorities and not according to bureaucratic protocol: shelter comes before amenity; walls and roof before electricity and a bath. In a very real way, the *barriadas* are now proving that the best and most satisfying low-cost housing, is in fact the cheapest. Hence the Peruvian government has even had a change of heart and is now beginning to support their development and ask architects such as Aldo Van Eyck, Christopher Alexander and James Stirling for their suggestions on aiding the 'Young Towns' as they are now approvingly called (66a, b).

(65) The next stages in *barriada* development are to fill out the places left for expansion and turn to more permanent construction.

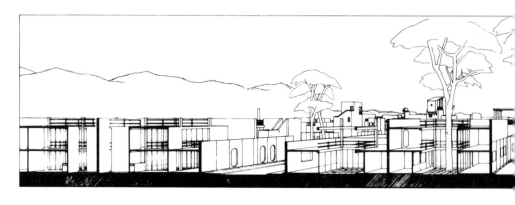

(66a) James Stirling
project for barriada development 1969: the perspective shows the architect-designed system which is first laid down and then added to by the individual builders with the traditional methods of construction.

(66b) James Stirling
plan of barriada development: four units clustered around a common service core can each expand by adding on rooms in the vacant L-shape.

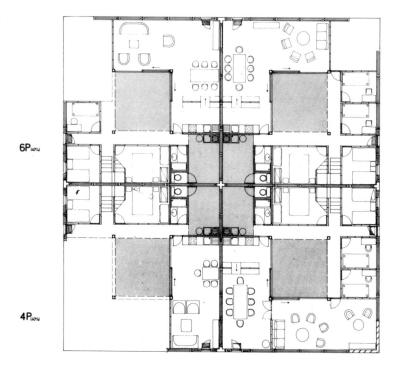

6P (units)

4P (units)

8P (20%)
CORNER AREA CAN BE
USED FOR EXTENSION OF
LIVING ROOM   BEDROOM
OR SHOP

8P+
CORNER AREA COMPLETED
BY HOUSE OWNER IN TRADITIONAL MATERIAL
FURTHER EXPANSION CAN TAKE
PLACE ON THE 1ST AND 2ND FLOOR

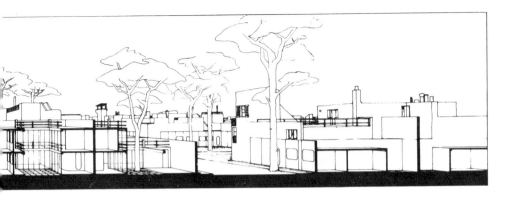

The reason for the recent popularity of *barriadas* in architectural circles is that they dramatize in a non-romantic way the opportunities for determining one's own way of life and life-style. Many other examples of this individual initiative could be given in the West, from the 'self-build' groups in England to 'Drop-City' in America (67), but none of them go to the extremes of the *barriadas* because the city authorities are much more adept at fighting off invasion and keeping the poor in their place. As some activist has said, the only way to get out of a Western ghetto is to burn your way out. There is no chance of occupying new land and the poor can only rent tenements from public housing authorities or from slum lords.

As yet, the students are the only minority group that have been able to organize effective protests against the present system. It is true that the Black Power Movement is organized and has disrupted cities by looting and burning, but it has not achieved the scale and ubiquity of disruption set in motion by the world-wide student movement. However, if black migration to cities continues at its present rate, one can predict such a concentration that there will be large-scale

(67) *Drop City*: geodesic domes made from automobile bodies are built by the local drop-out community in Arizona. Many forecasters predict the drop-out community as a major social alternative for the next thirty years.

1 Cohn-Bendit, *op. cit.* pp. 251–2

2 Few people put their finger on this cause, because the concept of 'power' is so discredited through its abuse; see Hannah Arendt *op. cit.*

3 Daniel Cohn-Bendit argues that continual non-leadership is *possible* and *desirable* but it seems to me it is neither; as to the former, it lasted only as long as there was police brutality; as to the latter, it would keep affairs on a fundamental level with, like the bureaucracy, no one responsible for anything. For his discussion of the police brutality as a catalyst see *op. cit.* pp. 57–9

urban riots in the US in the 1970s. In these the blacks and other oppressed minority groups will take over the cities for long periods and set up their own version of the French barricades of May. It is to this French movement and student power that I will confine my next remarks, because they show a pattern of minority revolt that could become a model for the future.

It appears that in spite of widespread talk about 'the oppressed masses', it is the minorities who feel the oppression and not the mythical, exploited working class. While the working class may be oppressed in some large, subconscious sense, most of the workers have accepted industrial-bourgeois values and hope to ameliorate working conditions within the traditional system through their official representatives such as the Communist Party and Trade Unions. This has been explicitly acknowledged both by the workers, who are very suspicious of the student revolutionaries and such student activists as Cohn-Bendit, who speak of the 'militant minorities'.[1]

It indeed makes much more sense to argue that only the minorities are alienated and, more radically, that in a specialized society, everyone, even the establishment, feels themselves, at one time or another, part of a repressed minority group. Andy Warhol's cryptic remark 'in the future everyone will be famous for fifteen minutes' means that everyone will be alienated for the rest of the time – when they are no longer famous or, more important, in a position to direct their political destiny. The system that all revolutionists are fighting against is one where power and self-determination have not been usurped by a conspiratorial class, but have simply ceased to exist. In a total bureaucracy, no conspirators exist anymore, no one is responsible for anything and the only thing that can be blamed for mistakes or inhumanity is 'the system'. It is this loss of power and self-determination which the revolutionists are fighting and which makes the spectacle of violence, the theatre of cruelty, the hippy love-ins and all the rest of it such an enjoyable affair for everyone, including the 'outraged' press (just one more

minority group). Alienation from power is total.[2]

The attempt to gain back power on a level where it is needed has not met with overwhelming success, but several examples can be cited. First of all there are the historical examples such as the anarchist communities in Barcelona of 1936–37, the Makhno Movement and the 'workers councils' set up right after the Russian Revolution. These various movements lasted for only a few years, before they lost power to the more usual forms of centralized governments. But while they did last, they proved that the anarchist principle of decentralized power was politically viable and socially desirable. More recently in France, the events of May 1968 have again proved this permanent possibility. Various Action Committees were formed which *directed the revolution* (if that is the right phrase) according to their own specific needs and situation. There was no centralized revolutionary party and, as long as the police were on the attack, no need for a leader or leadership.[3] There was just spontaneous organization and *ad hoc* aid coming from the people of Paris. After the 'events' had taken on a consistent pattern, street barricades of slightly used cars were constructed (68) and the Action Committees were formed. These met in continual discussion, were open to anyone, formulated general principles and took specific action suited to the situation at hand. Since the official means of communication were never taken over by the activists, they had to rely on their Action Committees to distribute information, publish the widely-read wall newspapers, and print, with the aid of architectural students in the Ecole des Beaux Arts, the posters of protest. The specific contribution of architectural students should not be overemphasized here, and yet, because of the strong Utopian tradition in architectural thinking, these students often played a greater role than those from other disciplines. In Italy, for instance, they were instrumental in starting the student protest and in Japan, Holland and America they were not far behind the first protagonists.

However, the important point is that the Action Committees came close to realizing the ideal of participatory democracy. Not only did they meet everyday and allow everyone to participate, vote and initiate policy, but each one was quite autonomous so that they could make up their own rules as they went along (horizontal rather than vertical organization). It is continually stressed that the virtue of these committees was their spontaneity; the fact that they came into being as a result of specific *action*, specific street battles, specific necessities such as food and shelter, as opposed to preconceived *ideas* on how a revolution should be made and its organizations set up. If anything, the 'non-leaders' of the revolt were especially suspicious of Marxist ideologies and the idea of a revolutionary party and vanguard élite. Most of their own polemics were concerned with showing how the Russian Revolution failed as soon as 'all power to the Soviets' was turned into 'all power to the (bureaucratic) party'. And the rest of their scorn was reserved for the Trade Unions and Communist Party who merely underwrote the bureaucratic organization and attacked their revolt, ultimately causing its downfall.

Thus these examples of specific *action* (the *barriada* invasion, the student protest, the May revolt etc.) have all started to explore alternatives to the present majority rule. They reject the idea of present democratic election as too insensitive, or in their words as 'the substitution of one set of gangsters for another set of gangsters every five years'. They propose to replace this majority system by a participatory democracy with elections as often as needed and with political and economic power resting most strongly in the smallest groups.

There are several present developments of both a technical and architectural nature which are likely to support these positions in the future. As already mentioned, on the technical side there now exists all the refined equipment of communication which could permit sensitive interaction between the individual and society (40). If a society wished, it could have a daily or even hourly referendum on any issue which allowed all people to vote. Every person could be

(68) *Street barricade in France* May 1968: an ultimate in expendable moving architecture. The piles of cars bear an ironic resemblance to car dumps of consumer society.

1 This kind of referendum and the equipment has been proposed by Dr V. K. Zworkin: see *The World in 1984*, Penguin Books, London, 1965 vol. 11

2 G. A. Miller, 'The magical number seven plus or minus two: some limits on our capacity for processing information'; *The Psychological Review*, vol. 60. pp. 81–97

3 Melvin Webber, 'The Urban Place and the Non Place Urban Realm' in *Explorations into Urban Structure*, ed. Webber *et al.*, University of Pennsylvania Press, 1964

equipped with a voting telephone and a radio which announced the specific referendum.[1] The difference between this proposal and the present voting system is that it would allow the voting to take place at home, that it could take place at a moment's notice, when the issues are still relevant, and that the results could be known within an hour of the referendum. While none of this would necessarily guarantee minority interests, at least it would make the present system more responsive to real majority desires – instead of them being a matter for speculation. But with the correct decentralized structure, it could also respond to minority interests in a sensitive way.

The recent architectural developments which favour these positions are of various kinds. On the most fundamental level is the recent emphasis by planners that any city is made up of a series of local areas or sub-systems (69). These sub-systems may or may not conform to local neighbourhoods, sub-cultures and physical boundaries, but they are the basic units by which we experience any city. That is to say, we remember and understand any city just as we understand any sequence of words; by subdividing it up into related and meaningful chunks.[2] The great problem is that with the increase in mobility and communication, these chunks are changing fast and may no longer correspond with previous subdivisions. There is thus a conflict between past functional and formal subsystems and emergent realities. A new community will emerge which finds neither physical expression nor political power.

In order to deal with these emergent situations, the planner Melvin Webber has invented the concept of the 'interest-community'.[3] This concept not only under-lines the fact that any modern metropolis is made up of a plurality of groups, but also the much more hidden situation that any individual is likely to be a member of many interest-communities and, moreover, that they may have nothing to do with specific location or place. In fact with the increase in mobility and communication, they are less likely to be tied to a specific place:

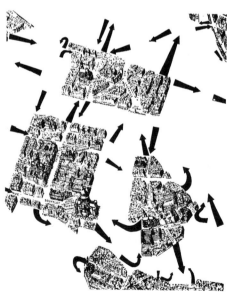

(69) **Guy Debord**
Situationist map of Paris
1961: any large metropolis is experienced as a series of semi-autonomous chunks, each with their own identity. These are the basic unit of urban experience and one navigates from chunk to chunk just as one cuts up continuous speech into a series of meaningful sub-sets.

'Spatial distribution is not the crucial determinant of membership in these professional societies, but interaction is. It is clearly no linguistic accident that "community" and "communication" share the Latin root *communis* in common. Communities comprise people with common interests who communicate with each other.'[1]

These interest-communities and those of the future will be increasingly formed on the basis of friendship, ideology and professional interest, and less on the traditional bases of propinquity, neighbourhood, family and social caste. Thus the typical urbanite will spend his day in contact with many different groups, passing from one to the next as fast as he can, figuratively speaking, change his clothes. This raises a crucial problem: one cannot change a city to suit a new situation as fast as one can change a suit and tie, so that urban forms are doomed to a kind of irrelevance or anachronistic existence. The response of architects to this problem has been to design a great deal of flexibility into their structures (29), propose a flexible structure itself (73) or else provide a plurality of fixed centres which could correspond to separate needs (70). This last alternative may be the best solution because it would give each minority group its own location and identity. But even if the polycentred city is recognized as the *formal* answer to the question of pluralism, there will remain the much greater problem of protecting and furthering the rights of the separate interest-communities.

To meet this problem, planners have started the movement called 'Advocacy Planning'.[2] First developed fully by Paul Davidoff in 1965, the concept of advocacy was taken over direct from legal practice and applied to urbanism. It was meant to supplant the idea that a planner would design for the whole community with its best interests in mind,

1 *Ibid*, p. 110

2 Paul Davidoff, 'Advocacy and Pluralism in Planning', *JAIP*, November 1965, and *Planning for Diversity and Choice*, ed. Stanford Anderson, MIT Press, Cambridge, Mass., 1968, with an excellent bibliography of books on the future

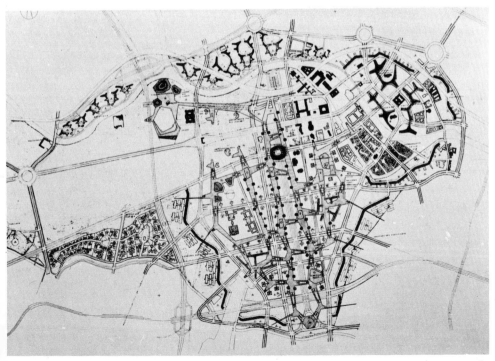

(70) **Alison** and **Peter Smithson** *Berlin Scheme* 1958: the large city of the future will be polycentred, gaining its identity through such fixes as a series of clustered centres, a wall of building and a pedestrian net.

by the idea that he should represent the special interest-group, just as a lawyer would represent his client's interests in court. The confrontation of many such advocates all pleading the minority interests which they represent, would lead more easily to these interests being satisfied than presently occurs under the majority system. For in the present system planners tend to avoid a strong defence of the good life as seen by a minority group and, even more, tend to avoid assuming positions which might threaten the *status quo* or their own, professional status within it. The result is that there is no effective advocate for the plurality of groups and thus their rights are sacrificed to the interests of the whole, or in revolutionist terms of the establishment. Advocacy Planning has grown

(71a, b) **Cedric Price** *Fun Palace* 1963: this servicing mechanism, really a gigantic erector set and toy box, allows the individual to pick out whatever arrangement and function he may desire, use it and then pack it away when no longer relevant. The large, travelling gantry crane is the only permanent object. For a built fun palace see pls. 18a, b, c.

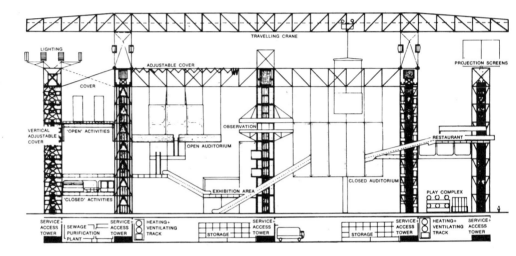

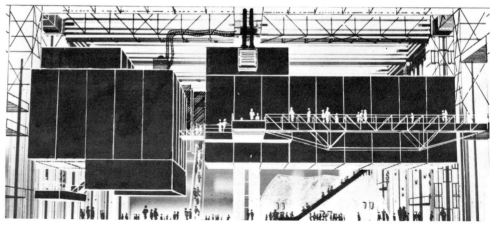

since its inception in the early 1960s into a fairly large movement with advocate groups now helping some poorer communities in Boston, Harlem, San Francisco, Syracuse and many other American cities. Basically these groups have aided blacks in the ghetto and poor urban whites in preparing renewal plans and in taking advantage of complex, bureaucratic aids; but the idea of advocacy can obviously be generalized across a whole pluralistic society, where often everyone's interests are sacrificed to some mythical good or general will.

No one has been so active as Jane Jacobs in showing that it is the habitual patterns of middle-class thought that are at fault here.[1] Professional planners and rationalist architects have continually mistaken statistical averages and supposedly universal norms for the more actual functioning of specific city systems – the street, or square or community – which can only be treated as complex, highly interrelated variables. Fortunately there now exist methods for dealing with these complex systems (which will be discussed under the logical tradition) so that one can foresee the richness and diversity of the old cities returning to the new. Yet if the pluralistic cities of the future are really to work, it will not be so much the result of these new methods but more due to the action of the minority groups themselves who have taken political and economic power into their own hands and made the city work.

The last, specifically architectural, contribution to the activist tradition is the idea of expendability (44). Cedric Price has developed it in a particular way, emphasizing its utilitarian nature. He contends that the main fault of cities and their organizations is that they continue to exist way beyond their functioning life and thereby exert a deadening effect on the present. All systems, all buildings, should therefore be designed *so that they last just so long as they are useful* and not a second more. The architect should specify the intended life-span of each system, build in obsolescence and make sure that all his structures are subject to quick change (71a, b). We recognize here the obvious parallel to the French activists who

1 Jane Jacobs *The Death and Life of Great American Cities*, Penguin Books, London, 1964, p. 460

(72a, b) **J. P. Jungmann**
Dyoden: for the Utopie
group's social commentary
see pl. 24.

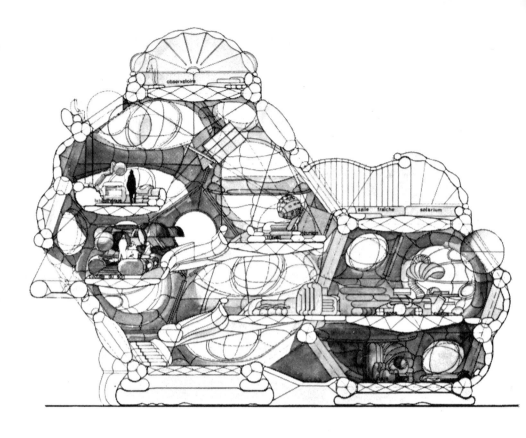

(73a, b) **J. P. Jungmann**
Dyoden.

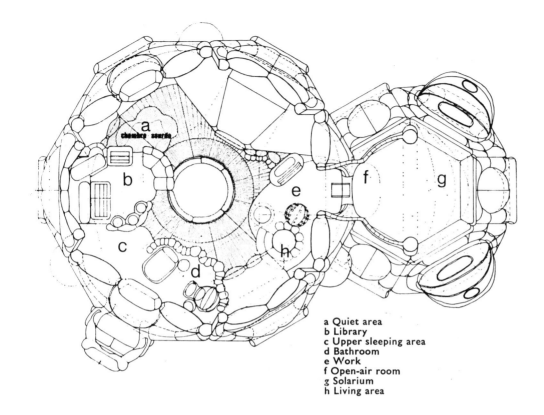

a Quiet area
b Library
c Upper sleeping area
d Bathroom
e Work
f Open-air room
g Solarium
h Living area

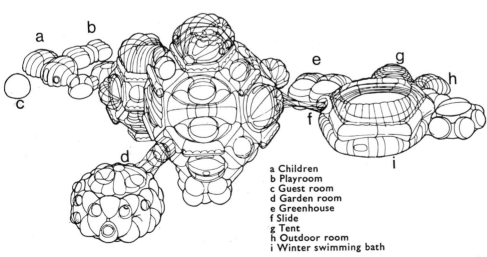

a Children
b Playroom
c Guest room
d Garden room
e Greenhouse
f Slide
g Tent
h Outdoor room
i Winter swimming bath

have an equal suspicion of all previous solutions and wish to transcend the limits of the past.

In fact the French *Utopie* group has translated these ideas of expendability and social utility into a very striking kind of architecture based on pneumatic structures (72a, b; 73a, b). They have designed pneumatic projects where everything is inflatable and disposable including the walls, floor, furniture, joints, structure, skin and even mechanical equipment. Physically the results resemble M. Bibendum, the Michelin Man, with his body made up of bulbous tires. Functionally the concept is very responsive as it allows easy transport, quick erection (74) and sudden disposability at the prick of a needle. Tactilely, the blow-up is the most comfortable and friendly support, apart from that of sitting on another human body, a fact not usually appreciated (75). And socially, the *Utopie* group has shown that pneumatic structures are as responsive as

clothing, they can be altered to suit the situation as fast as it changes, and thus avoid the continual irrelevance of more permanent structures.

All these factors of the activist tradition – from the student revolt to expendability – do not yet add up to a movement strong enough to completely realize the goals that are pursued. Yet in a very real sense, the activist tradition is the power house of architecture, the most dynamic of all the traditions, because of its continual insistence on transcending realities as they exist. If at present the activists only accomplishment is their domination of discussion and the news media, they can take some solace from the fact that indirectly this will have a powerful influence on all the other traditions and bend their action toward more radical ends. Furthermore, with the proliferation of the information media, the activists will see their substantive criticisms becoming more widely disseminated in the 1970s. If there is not the

(74) **American Airlines** *Astrosphere*: dual-walled dome built up of tubular segments; inflation time for the building two hours.

(75) *Blow-up furniture*, the closest support to the human body.

cataclysmic revolution which they desire, there is much more likely to be a permanent, indirect revolution with many of their ideas being co-opted, borrowed, plagiarised and answered by others. Since the activist tradition shares with the intuitive the great power of imagining new conditions which transcend the present, there is a natural, although unstable, affinity between the two. If we refer back to the evolutionary tree (p. 46), we can see how the two overlap on such specific issues as a 'responsive environ-ment' and more autonomy for minority groups.

In the 1990s these two traditions may well coalesce into the Biomorphic School and emerge as the strongest, single movement at the end of the twentieth century, for many of the breakthroughs which are predicted in biology and automation will satisfy the desire of both traditions for more personal autonomy and freedom.

7 The intuitive tradition

(Pop – fashion – plug-in – responsive – Biomorphic – personalized – underwater – telechiric – chimeric)

(76) **Hans Hollein** interior of *Retti Candle Shop* Vienna 1965: sheets of polished aluminium with their natural silver hue; even the mechanical equipment is presented as a jewel.

The intuitive tradition, like the activist, is always looking outside architecture into other fields, hoping to find something it can borrow and re-use to transform the present. This continual ransacking of the cultural cupboard for anything pertinent obviously makes for eclecticism and a certain superficiality. Ideas and forms are stolen from fashion, movies, comic books, deep-sea diving, space exploration, technology, biology, robotology, and even chimericology, a field which may come into existence in order to study those hybrid monsters – half men, half beast – which might become possible by the year 2000.

Anything is acceptable so long as it is slightly interesting, different from the present and exotic. Thus science fiction writers tend to fertilize the tradition and many architectural forecasters, such as Michel Ragon,[1] simply base their predictions on what is different but possible, such as living underground or under water. Thus it is easy to criticize this tradition for its naivety; for its assumption that what is technically possible will become socially acceptable and be diffused throughout a society. In fact, from the billions of technical break-throughs, there are only a few such as the radio or automobile which become so ubiquitous that they transform the environment. Nevertheless, the intuitive tradition, by sheer dint of endless speculation, manages to hit on these few, get excited about them and show their social potential, a potential which would otherwise remain largely undeveloped. It is the early-warning system and avant-garde of the possible. It is also where the avant-garde is mostly located. And since this group often tends toward the extreme of gratuitous change, the intuitive tradition tends to break away from the activist and join up with the self-conscious (see evolutionary tree) on their common ground of fashion. This is why, for instance, the *Utopie* group criticizes the Archigram group (24), when otherwise they have much in common.

If one glances through the architectural magazines of the world, one often gets the impression that there is an élite group of style-conscious popinjays whose sole desire is to provide each other with a surfeit of visual delectations. The architect's love for form, form as an end in itself, is so strong and ubiquitous that there really is an international group who follow and perform for each other and the 'glossies'. Yet this group is not as frivolous as it might at first appear, because through its delight in manipulating form, it does as much to alleviate industrial squalor and the general dampening of the senses as do the activists. Contrary to the omnipresent trend in all industrial nations towards the bland and soporific, this group actually heightens sensual awareness – sometimes even to a state of frenzied palpitation, to

1 Michel Ragon, who had at last count, three books on the future of architecture: *Ou Vivrons-Nous Demain?* Laffont, Paris, 1963; *Les Cités de L'Avenir*, Planete, Paris, 1965; *La Cité de L'An 2000*, Casterman, Paris, 1968

(77) **Hans Hollein** exterior
of *Retti Candle Shop*
Vienna 1965: instead of
advertising its product the
shop invites inspection by
offering brief glances
through a homogenous
wall of polished
aluminium.

the threshold of aesthetic pain. 'It's so beautiful it's killing me', is a not uncommon reaction. There are so many architects in this group, from the Dolce Vita school in Milan to the Catalan rebels in Spain, that I will confine my remarks to the most rigorous: to those whose pursuit of the obsessive image is so complete and dedicated that one can say their pursuit of fashion is uncorruptible and of the highest integrity.

Perhaps the most luxuriant of all their confections is the candle shop in Vienna by the architect Hans Hollein (76, 77). This very small, two-room shop was designed to display candles in a hieratic way that reminds one of Egyptian funerary chapels. Not only does the plan pulsate in a series of semi-enclosed spaces and recessed niches which withhold quick fulfillment and invite further exploration, but the surfaces – highly polished and

(78a, b) **Ricardo Bofill** and Partners *Xanadu* Calpe, Spain 1967: this complex of seventeen apartments is set against an untouched landscape of mountain and sea.

(79) **Ricardo Bofill** and Partners *Valpineda Plug-in*: ninety units are plugged *into* structural brick cores and steel columns. These 'mother' units are then allowed further elements to be plugged *on to* them. The *ad hoc* construction consists of such things as road drainage pipes used for window openings.

(80) **Ron Herron** *Walking City* 1963: a city which could carry society to any point in the world on telescoping legs (compare with pl. 41).

anodized aluminium – set up ambiguous effects which arouse curiosity through their endless shimmering reflections. Such obsessive care and precision have gone into the detailing, that even the mechanical equipment begins to look like the jewels of Tutankhamen. And yet what is all this suggestive veiling and passionate precision for – a little hole in the wall that sells lumps of wax. This disproportion between function and form, or programme and image, is quite common in the modern world and has been since the nineteenth century. One can see the urban forces, which produce it, even growing in strength in the future with the increase in leisure and information media, so that the opportunities for fashion will also grow equally.

Similar kinds of anomalies occur in Italy and Spain, where even socially conscious architects end up by designing expensive pleasure palaces for want of better commissions. In fact the young architect Ricardo Bofill, a frequent protester against social conditions in Spain, has designed a pleasure dome called Xanadu (78a, b). This work, like all his

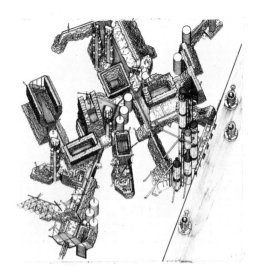

(81) **Peter Cook** *Plug-in City* 1964: a basic extendable structure serviced by railways, helicopters and hovercraft. All the plug-in units are easily clipped into place and can be dissected and discarded when obsolete.

others, achieves a very interesting resolution between exuberant forms and necessary functions: the cascade of cubic rooms descends around a central service spine; the alternating setbacks provide the necessary shade; the hyperbolic roofs allow better views. Each one of the seemingly arbitrary shapes is carefully thought out and beautifully constructed in a way that recalls the rational expressionism of Gaudi, whose influence on Bofill and others in Barcelona is still strong. While these two architects of the intuitive tradition are so formally conscientious as to remain uncorruptible, many others are likely to make their peace in the future with whatever political regimes happen to exist, because of the usual political neutrality in the intuitive tradition and because of the structural affinity between fashion and hierarchical societies.

The group that has been more active than any other in projecting *images* of the future is the London based Archigram group. Starting off with monumental images of mechanized cities, what they call 'hardware' (80, 81), they have now moved in the direction of 'software' environments – systems of environmental control that aid personal choice and are responsive to

(82) **Archigram** *Control and Choice* 1967: an environment of responsive systems such as extendable structures, movable pneumatic skins, adjustable walls and floors, service robots and collapsible electric cars which turn into bedrooms!

(83) **Archigram** *Instant City* 1969: the translation of light and sound through electric media means that a city can be created and dissolved in an instant. Instant City is really like a travelling circus which would visit different towns in the provinces and involve participants in creating different events. The hardware is made up of tension nets held by balconies, travelling cranes, telescoping robots, projective screens and neon signs recalling Las Vegas.

individual whim and desire (82–4). However in both the hardware and software projects one principle has remained the same: the plug-in idea, or the idea that various systems are semi-autonomous and change at different rates. Thus Plug-in City consists of a basic structure with a forty-year life span, which holds movement systems on a twenty-year cycle and houses which can be relocated and clipped on every fifteen years. Archigram's clip-on idea, previously called dissectibility, is as much a result of their creative method as their philosophy, because they clip-on (steal) ideas from every possible source: bug-eyed monsters from science fiction (80), tubular blobs from oil-refineries (81), tele-scoping robot walls from comic books (82, 84), and tension nets and space-frames from the architectural tradition (83). But all this thievery has a valuable point. It calls attention to, and exploits, the vast range of independent services which already exist. Most architects would rather not know about these services, which now take up half the cost of modern building, or if they do acknowledge them, they are usually given monumental expression. However Archigram manages to make an architecture of the services alone, an architecture that dramatizes consumer choice, an architecture which more than any other captures the poetry inherent in an advanced industrial civilization. If men are to find significance in the machine, it will come through the sheer pleasure of manipulating and dramatizing it, a pleasure which is manifest in and communicated by all Archigram's works, particularly as they leave all their thievery undisguised for everyone to understand and enjoy.

The idea of the totally responsive environment and the idea of stealing, from one source or another, combined and reached an infamous crescendo in the movie *Barbarella*. Originally a comic strip about a future love-goddess and her 'sexploits', it was first taken up by the *Kultur-Kritiks* and analyzed in depth for its not-too-hidden significance for current *mores*; then it was made into a movie farce, a camp pastiche of science-fiction thrillers with their Positronic Ray Guns and The Excessive Machine (a

(84) **Archigram** *Living Area* 1990: the usual gadgets of the future, service robots, hoverchair, inflatable floors and ultrasonic cooking equipment. Because it is more economic to move things than people and because of the increase in specialized industries such as electronics, it may well be that the future home will take over many functions of today's factory.

1 Reyner Banham, 'Triumph of Software', in *New Society*, 31 October 1968

machine which tries to kill Barbarella with pleasure, but impotently blows its fuses instead); and finally it was reinterpreted by the architectural critic Reyner Banham as the 'Triumph of Software' and thus had its impact on the architectural scene. From French comic strip to *Kulturkritik*, to Italo-American cinema to English architecture all in a few years – a real case of McLuhanite information implosion if there ever was one. But its lesson for the future of architecture was not just its retranslation through many media in the 'world village', but more the fact that it gave the first real image of a biomorphic architecture (86) and the triumph of software (Barbarella) over hardware (the excessive machine). Not only did it show the usual inflatable structures being sat upon, bounced upon, slithered through and caressed but it also introduced the fur-lined spaceship (85) which was so excessively comfortable and comforting that it was a singular pleasure for Barbarella to crash land in it and be jostled and tossled about:

'Of all the 'materials friendly to man' (fur) is the friendliest, because is it kissing cousin to our surface and grows in some of our friendliest places. But it also has, in the most objective and quantifiable terms, physical properties that would make it worth inventing if it did not exist: flexible, shock-

(85) *Barbarella* in her fur-lined spaceship.

absorbing, heat-insulating, acoustically absorbent and selectively responsive to reflecting light.'[1]

In the future substitutes for fur, skin and other anthropomorphic effects will proliferate until it will be quite possible for everyone to have a responsive environment: 'friendly to look at and pleasing to touch', as the advertisement for mink puts it. In fact in anticipating future developments in biology and automation, it would be reasonable to assert that in *one* sense the environment will become more and more friendly, anthropomorphic, humane and will be built, literally, to the human scale. Designers of robots, for instance, find that it makes more sense to give these machines human dimensions and actions so that they can navigate through a human world than change the world to suit the robots.[1]

Furthermore, when biology becomes the major metaphor of the 1990s, the intuitive tradition will explode in a burst of biomorphic images suited to the individual and organic development. Already the Biomorphic School has had a long, but fitful, history reaching a high point in the beginning of this century with the work of Antonio Gaudi and Frank Lloyd Wright and later oscillating in strength with the work of Soleri, Goff, Kiesler, Scharoun, the Metabolists, Johansen, Rodilla, O'Gorman, Couelle, Hausermann, Bloc, Katavolos, Guedes, Doernach and, even at times, Le Corbusier. I mention this long list to emphasize the fact that the Biomorphic School is already a strong movement although its members ordinarily work alone and are, for the most part, unaware of being part of a tradition. The work and philosophy of Soleri are typical of it. Usually built by hand out of poured concrete or rammed earth his work grows organically according to individual needs and desires, incorporating elements from any source whether they be man-made or natural. The advantages of this biomorphic approach are, of course, that it is custom-made to the circumstances and, with technical advances such as sprayed concrete, increasingly economical. Further advances in chemicals, plastics and glues will no doubt

(86) *Barbarella* 1968: life in the labyrinth is a biomorphic existence where men have actually merged with the contours of the earth and the human forms of dead vegetation. In the background is the hardware city of Sogo, the city of evil, where the architecture is still ancient steel and glass.

make this personalized kind of building even more cheap and easy. One can imagine spraying a house out of a shaving can and then dissolving it away with a vaporizer.

Soleri's philosophy, which tends to be linked with the Biomorphic School, is based on the ideas of evolutionary growth put forward by Julian Huxley, Teilhard de Chardin and others. Like these philosophers of evolution, he stresses ecological balance and the emergence of the psycho-social order, what he calls the 'Cultural Mind', made up of the totality of ideas and social organizations which are super-imposed on the vegetal and animal orders. Soleri integrates these orders in a gigantic whole which recalls organic growths and is called, half ironically, Babel, after that visionary megastructure which was also never finished (87). Many architects of the Biomorphic School such as Doernach and Katavolos have imagined organic-like structures being erected from chemical reactions and placed on or under the sea.

1 See the whole issue devoted to machines of *Science Journal* October 1968, especially Isaac Asimov's 'The Perfect Machine' pp. 115–18; his 'three laws of robotics' are being literally applied in industry

(87) **Paolo Soleri** *Babel II*
1968: this tree-like city is
divided into four residential
levels suspended around a
central core which contains
communal space and
internal parks. Light and
air penetrate to the centre
through climatic controls
and over the hanging
gardens of building.

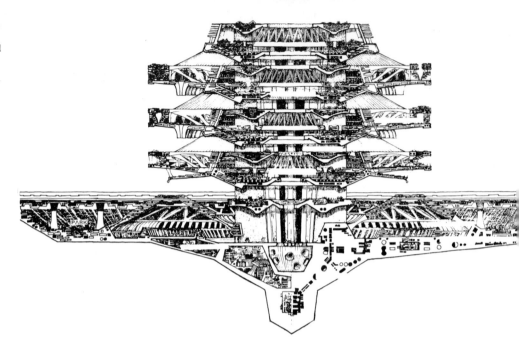

(88) **Eduard Albert** and
Commandant Cousteau
Floating Island 1967:
inspired by marine biology
structures many architects
are projecting semi-
detachable floating cities
rather than permanent
megastructures such as
Tange's Tokyo Bay Scheme.
Compare with pls. 41, 59,
80.

The sea has always exerted a strong fascina-
tion for the intuitive tradition because it is
the last place on earth still undomesticated by
man and still relatively dangerous. Most of
man's future relations with the sea will be on
top of it (88) and not under it because of the
inhospitable conditions which exist at great
depth: it takes a certain 'decompression
time' to transfer between the surface and the
deep and it is very dark, quiet, lonely and
claustrophobic at great depths. Food lacks
taste, smells are undetectable, coffee cools as
soon as heated, toast is likely to explode and
when one person manages to talk to another
he invariably has the cackle of Donald Duck,
due to the necessarily high helium content of
the air. But if one can't imagine that large
colonies of men will soon live underwater,

one can imagine the continual exploration of the sea for its protein and mineral resources. France, the United States and Russia have all set up extensive programmes to exploit the great wealth that lies underwater. Since 70 per cent of the earth is covered by water and 80 per cent of animal and vegetable life is under it, it is obvious what this 'exploitation' could mean in material terms. Sea farming and sea mining will become major industries if the earth's resources are ever diminished beyond a certain point. The kind of hardware or architecture that will exist to explore these new resources will bear a certain resemblance to the submarine, from which they have been evolved, but will also have numerous detectors such as television eyes, sonar beams and arm-like devices to pick up and manipulate the material (89a, b). If the underwater vehicle does not become as common as the automobile is today at least these arm-like devices are likely to proliferate in a number of roles. Classified under the general term 'telechiric' (from the Greek for 'distant hand'), these devices were first brought into use where men had to manipulate such untouchable things as radioactive material from a distance. Already their use has been extended to helping the physically disabled, explorations underwater and in outer space (97), and work in the factory (102). Indeed several forecasters predict that the house robot will become an addition to this list by the year 2000, but it will still be used mainly for industrial and military purposes.

For instance, the exoskeleton and CAM (Cybernetic Anthropomorphic Machine) were developed for the United States Army in order to move large explosives over difficult terrain (90, 91). Not only can these telechiric devices amplify man's strength by a factor of twenty-five, but they are also designed to walk over obstacles that would intimidate any tank. However there was one obstacle caused by the mechanism itself. When directed to push a tack into a heavy wall, it pushed the whole wall down instead. In order to make the mechanism less obtuse and more refined, the action of 'force feedback' was built into it, so that the operator could feel any pressures it was exerting on the environment. The arms and legs of the machine are thus true extensions of the operators' own arms and, in effect, he is able

6000 POUNDS
OF SCIENTIFIC
EQUIPMENT PAYLOAD

1. STERN ACCESS TRUNK
2. VERTICAL PROPULSION MOTOR
3. T.V. MONITOR
4. FORWARD SONAR DISPLAY
5. GYROCOMPASS
6. DECK SUPERSTRUCTURE
7. BOW ACCESS TRUNK
8. BOW ACCESS HATCH
9. SCANNING C.T.F.M. SONAR
10. EXTENSIBLE ILLUMINATOR
11. T.V. CAMERA & ILLUMINATOR
12. MANIPULATOR DEVICE
13. OBSERVER
14. OXYGEN FLASK
15. PORT ILLUMINATOR
16. BATTERY
17. SIDE-LOOKING SONAR
    (UNDER BALLAST TANK)
18. KEEL SUPERSTRUCTURE
19. SHOT BALLAST SOLENOID
20. SKIPPER
21. BALLAST TANK
22. PORT PROPULSION MOTOR
23. STERN ACCESS HATCH

(89a, b) *Aluminaut* 1964: the typical underwater vehicle used for salvage and rescue operations, such as the search for the H-bomb lost off the Spanish coast, as well as mining etc. The 9 ft articulated arms are capable of lifting 200 lbs each. The vehicle is also equipped with various sensing devices and is capable of 3·5 knots speed.

(90) **General Electric** *Hardiman* 1966: this exoskeleton amplifies man's strength to perform difficult tasks such as loading and unloading 1500 lb bombs.

(91) **General Electric** *CAM* 1969: an extension of the man-amplifier (left) but more like the 'walking truck' which can walk over rough terrain or climb obstacles as shown here. The front legs are controlled by the operator's arms and the back legs by his legs, all on the principle of 'force feedback', i.e , pressures on the machine are felt as pressures on his limbs.

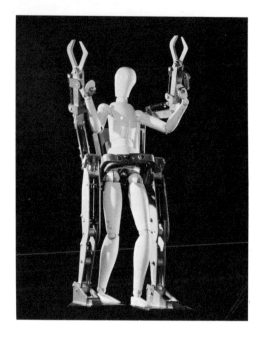

to feel his environment as if in direct contact with it.

The development of the exoskeleton combined with the development of the air-conditioned suit (92) led to a project where

(92) Man in air-conditioned space suit using telechiric devices called 'master-slave manipulators', devices often used to manipulate dangerous material.

finally the architecture became as responsive as clothing – in fact became a form of bulky clothing itself (93). This project of Michael Webb, as well as the work done on telechiric devices, points towards the goal of achieving a really delicate relation between man and machine that has been desired for a long time. Finally machines are now capable of sensing and responding immediately to any movement or nerve impulse in man. The time is not far off before they become a ubiquitous part of his environment and the first true Cyborgs (cybernetic organisms) are created – part man, part machine. These will rival the Chimera (part man, part animal) in raising opportunities and dangers for the future. Both will become feasible by the 1990s and both will be ransacked by the intuitive tradition for all their extensive implications. Obviously when machines, animals, and man reach such a state of interdependence, our view of all three will change in radical ways – a point to which I will return in conclusion. However I must first discuss briefly the last two traditions which have a mutual affinity and tend to be opposed to the intuitive.

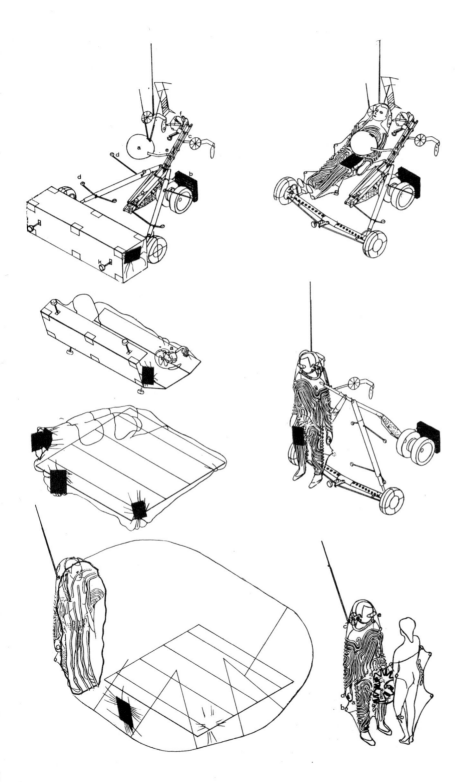

(93) **Michael Webb** (of Archigram group) *Suitaloon* 1968: the exoskeleton plus liquid-conditioned suit plus inflatable room plus the plug-in concept finally produces a house which is really just clothing.

(94a) **Frei Otto** *West German Pavilion* Expo 67: the tension net with its most economic distribution of structural forces.

(94b) **Kenzo Tange** *Theme Pavilion* Expo 70: a giant megastructure with moving lighting booms and loudspeakers on telescoping arms shelters a performance robot (carrying people). All the images and ideas which Archigram projected six years ago have been rationalized and strained through the systematic design process of the Japanese.

8 The logical tradition

(Parametric-megaform – space colonial – asteroids – ultra-light)

If the intuitive tradition becomes excited about the developments offered by science and technology, and thereby shows their social potential, the logical tradition either initiates them or treats them in a systematic way. Because of this rigour, the logical tradition has a certain moral authority not found in the other traditions and a contempt for anything which appears as fashion. It is public, open to criticism and directly answerable to specific demands. In fact in the 'age of science', those having access to systematic knowledge are often regarded with awe and assumed to have a monopoly on moral authority, if not on truth itself. They include the responsible engineer; the unequivocal scientist; and the man in touch with universal, cosmological forces. There has not been a *modern* architect who has not appealed to a 'universal law' or 'scientific truth' sometime in his career. In fact the idea of modern architecture is so closely connected with the abstract and 'verifiable' virtues of the engineer, that nearly everyone identifies it with such things as suspension bridges, tension nets (94a) and large, geometric mega-structures (94b). Because these aspects are so well known and because the Megaform School has already been mentioned (pp. 72–73), I will confine these remarks to only two aspects of the logical tradition: the Parametric School and Space Colonial.

The Parametric School has, if not in name then at least in numbers, the largest academic following of any of the present movements. Nearly every architecture school has some course devoted to cybernetic, systematic or, at least, rational design. While there are a variety of models, they all follow, in very general terms, the same overall method of 'divide and conquer'. The environmental problem is first identified and broken down into its smallest elements or parameters. Next these parameters are cleansed of their semantic weighting or cultural overtones, so that the designer is as free as possible from preconceptual bias. Then the relations between parameters are established and synthesized into sub-sets, which are in turn synthesized into a designed whole that is, in fact, the solution to the original problem. The only step I have left out is the very difficult one of translating each sub-set into a form diagram or a physical model.

While this method of design has been outlined by Christopher Alexander[1] for environmental problems, it obviously applies to any kind of design including such things as sending a man to the moon and back. From this example one gets an idea of how many billions of parameters have to be analyzed and coordinated over a ten-year period and how inadequate would be anything less than the systematic design method that was in fact followed. It is probably equally true that any problem as complex as

1 Of his many works, the two most relevant are *Notes on the Synthesis of Form*, Harvard University Press, Cambridge, Mass., 1964, and 'A City is not a Tree', *Design* February 1966

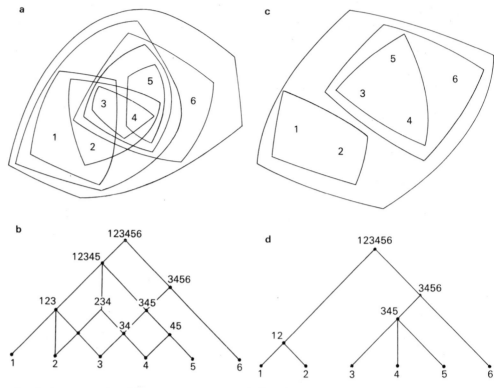

(95) Semi-lattice, to the left, compared with tree, to the right: the former corresponds to organic cities which have grown in linkage and diversity over time, while the latter represents the modern city which lacks this diversity and overlap.

1 The five immediate ones are (1) how can we be sure that we have the smallest, atomic parameters; (2) the right ones; (3) a complete set; (4) the right relations; (5) the right form diagrams and subsets? Even if these questions could be answered (which is impossible) there would still remain two nagging doubts: (6) moral questions tend to disappear in systematic design; (7) Shakespeare couldn't have written Hamlet if he had to start with such atomistic parameters as one melancholic Dane, one Oedipus Complex . . . Obviously some creations are best when saturated with associative links and not cleansed of their semantic weighting

city design must also follow this parametric method. While undoubtedly it has serious drawbacks,[1] it does provide the answer for dealing with highly complex city systems – the kind of problems in 'organized complexity' which Jane Jacobs has analysed and shown to elude the professional planners' kind of thinking in terms of statistical averages. Christopher Alexander also shows in his article 'A City is not a Tree' how this kind of thinking produces 'tree-like' cities, cities where the sub-sets are so autonomous that they lack the kind of rich diversity found in older towns (95). The problem is, among other things, mainly conceptual, because thought imposes its categories and then these categories impose isolated physical entities which do not relate or have very little overlap with each other. A Roman army camp with its rigid divisions is another tree-like system, whereas a successful dinner party with everyone conversing coherently is a semi-lattice. If the modern city is to have the richness and life which

106

characterize the old city then architects will have to provide this complex overlap with the aid of parametric methods.

As already mentioned, the prime reason for systematic design is that it alone can handle a great amount of complex requirements. Nowhere are they greater than in space exploration and so it is natural that this field has produced the epitome of parametric design. The results are always clear, precise, purist and eighteenth-century. That is they always have that cool, ascetic quality which speaks of self-discipline and a clear separation between nature and culture (96, 97). No one would dare design a messy, rusty spacecraft or defile an untouched planet with advertisement and urban detritus. All the space cities of the artists and actual designers appear as the oldest Utopian dreams of man: the well ordered city with all systems working exactly on command according to reason and precise calculation. Partially this is a result of necessity, since a mistake or unpremeditated act would be quickly fatal. But also the psychic forces of colonizing space should not be underrated, since they point to the eternal desire to start again in a new environment without the preconceptions and entanglements of the past. The imminent possibility of having many space stations on prolonged journeys into the unknown (98, 99) means that men will once again explore an untouched, potentially hostile nature where they can set up local islands cut off from previous civilization. Although this dream of the Utopian island completely isolated and secure from its mother community can be seen as an infantile form of escapism, it can also be seen as a mature form of returning to the scale of asking cosmological questions. It is probably both. In the second case, there are likely to be fundamentally new discoveries on such subjects as reversible time, antimatter, quarks, and gravity waves, as well as the most general question of all, the creation of the universe. Currently, the Big Bang, the Steady State and the Steady Bang are all competing theories which make their exits and re-entries with increasing speed. The next thirty years promises to be so saturated with scientific discoveries that cosmological watching, like star-gazing, will become a popular sport to be included in every fun palace (71).

(96) *2001 – A Space Odyssey*: the hardware in this movie is in the old classical, streamform tradition and is based on actual projects of the space programme.

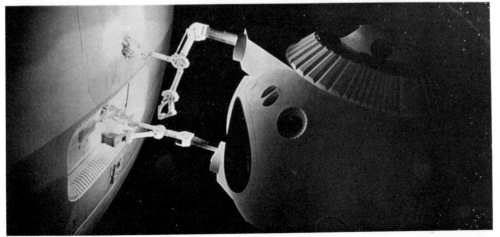

(97) *2001 – A Space Odyssey*: space-pod with its telechiric devices leaving its mother ship. Compare the purist hardware of these images with the first software space venture *Barbarella* (pls. 85, 86).

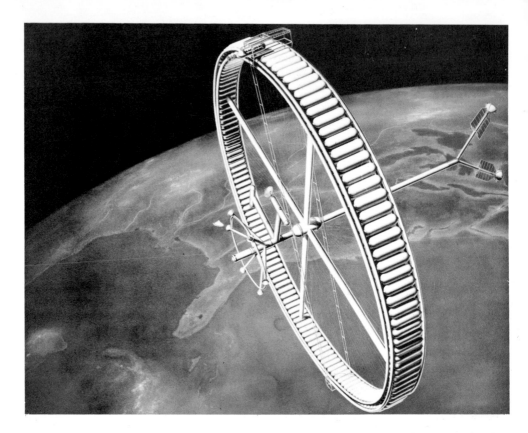

(98) **Lockheed Missiles and Space Company**
Space City 1990: the giant revolving wheel contains offices, laboratories and living quarters. Again compare the typical purist imagery of this hardware scheme with *Barbarella* pls. 85, 86).

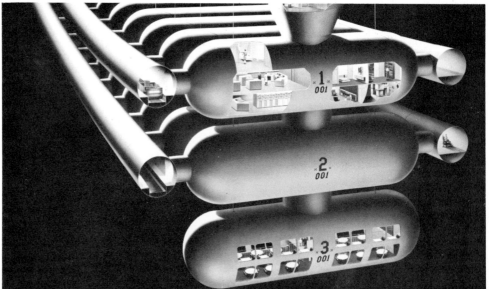

(99) **Lockheed Missiles and Space Company**
Home from Home 1990: shows how people might live and work in the Space City.

9 The idealist tradition

(Metaphysical – cybernetic – automated – semiological – significant)

With all these competing theories and ideas, not to mention competing minorities, the proliferation of different life-styles will become so confusing to the urban inhabitant that it will be even more necessary to design a comprehensible environment to help explain this diversity. The idealist tradition with its attention to expressive functionalism, symbolism and propriety will continue to serve these ends. In fact the idealist tradition is probably the *locus classicus* of modern architecture. It is the tradition which most architects align themselves with and hence it produces what has been called 'architect's architecture'; that is, buildings which are so specifically attuned to the nuance of environmental meaning that probably only trained architects can fully appreciate their subtleties. In any case, forms express their functions not because this is logical or inevitable, but rather because idealist architects take every care to make the forms comprehensible (100a, b, c, d). The architect James Stirling is perhaps the most representative of this tradition, not only because his works are the most functionally expressive, but also because like every other architect in this tradition he was greatly influenced by Le Corbusier, who projected the ideal of the environment made visible and comprehensible. In addition to Le Corbusier's *Ville Radieuse*, there is the project for Algiers (101) which remains one of the most convincing expressions of a skyscraper – that is a

vertical city with just as much content and diversity as the horizontal ones of the past. Apart from making these diverse functions articulate, Le Corbusier also continued to pose the question of their appropriateness. Like the activist, he relentlessly asked the moral question 'should the function exist?' and then the further one 'if so, in what proportion to the other functions?'

This interrogation of social content is central to the idealist tradition and has been formulated by the Goodmans as the ancient Greek ideal of 'neo-functionalism'.[1] They cross-examine the necessity and value of the functions themselves, not just their formal expression. And then, instead of proposing single solutions with fixed goals, they put forward *a set of alternative schemes* with the various goals made manifest enough for the individual to select what he wants. This idea of presenting clear alternative proposals is, of course, also the idea behind this book and the underlying concept of Bertrand de Jouvenel's *futuribles* or 'future possibles'.[2] In fact, if a movement towards thinking in terms of *futuribles* rather than inevitable fate or the single road does develop, then it is likely to evolve from the idealist tradition because of its long interest in ideal possibilities.

Before discussing some ways in which this tradition will make the 'information rich society' more intelligible, I will mention in

1 See Percival and Paul Goodman, *Communitas*, Vintage Books, New York, 1960, p. 19

2 See his *The Art of Conjecture, op. cit.*

(100a), **James Stirling and Michael Wilford** *Cambridge Faculty of History* 1968: the functions which are delineated include, from left to right, the book stacks, the glass-enclosed reading room, the surrounding corridors, the various teaching rooms descending in size from the top and the staircase and lift towers. All the glass walls are serviced by a travelling, cleaning boat.

(100b) *Cambridge Faculty of History* 1968: bird's-eye axonometric.

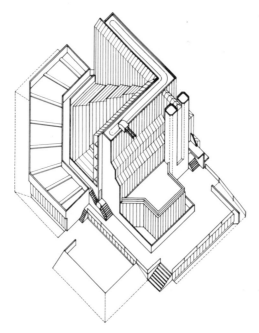

passing the Cybernetic School which has already started to exist. Of the many new possibilities which it is creating, such as computer design, data banks, holographic three-dimensional design and laser communications, I will only discuss the one which could have the greatest effect on the environment: automated production.

Ever since the Industrial Revolution, there has been a legitimate abhorrence of monotonous repetition caused by machines working with invariant programmes such as fixed moulds and set action patterns. One of the major tenets of modern architecture, sanctioned by Le Corbusier and Walter Gropius,

(100c) *Cambridge Faculty of History* 1968: entrance, faculty left, students right.

(100d) *Cambridge Faculty of History* 1968: reading room with extract units.

(101) **Le Corbusier** *Algiers skyscraper* 1938. The articulation of function creates not only a plastic symphony of visual delight, but a way of making the vertical city as comprehensible as the horizontal.

(102) (*right*) *Unimate* the industrial robot: the telechiric device coupled with a memory system means that mass production no longer has to be based on unvarying archetypes but can change endlessly with varying demand and resultant programming. The machine can be taught its job in one lesson if taken by its 'hand' and led through the required positions.

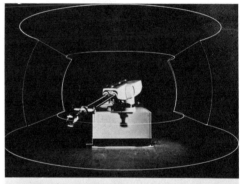

1 The literature is so large on this subject that any single citation would be rather arbitrary. Among others see the work of Durkheim, Wirth, Reismann, Whyte etc.

2 See Marshall McLuhan, *Understanding Media*, Sphere Books, London, 1967, p. 379–81

3 See *Meaning in Architecture*, ed. George Baird and Charles Jencks, George Braziller, New York, 1969; Barrie and Jenkins, London, 1970. The first five articles consider semiology and its relation to architecture

take over the tending and manipulating of other machines. It has the advantage over human labour of being more precise, stronger, more subject to heat and danger and almost indefatigable. But the specific relevance of the industrial robot to architecture means that the House of the Future (103) can be constructed as an automobile with every panel different and the joints moulded to suit the individual situation. The Smithsons' project of this name resembles a car's body in other ways too: all the surfaces are made up of jointed, curvilinear sections which allow easy cleaning by an electrostatic dust collector.

was that the architect should design invariant archetypes, 'standards' or *objet-types* which would then be endlessly repeated by mass production for a whole society. The justification was economic, sociological and Darwinian. The last justification I shall return to in conclusion, but the first two are relevant here because developments in automation and sociology have largely rendered them obsolete.

On the one hand, sociologists have shown that the *anomie* and conformity which have come from standardization are largely destructive of personal, social relations,[1] while on the other, prophets of automation[2] have indicated that the present cybernetic production can return us to the organic, handicrafted world where every form is different from the next at the same cost, speed and efficiency as repeated production. Because of telechiric machines which act as the craftsman's hands and cybernetic machines which act as his changeable mind, we *could* return to a totally custom-built world as far as the production process is concerned. The industrial robot (102) can be led through its paces just once by the factory hand and then

In so far as cybernetic production or the Second Industrial Revolution, as it is called, has an effect on the environment, it will return it to the pre-industrial past of the custom-built world. It is, however, the effect of ideas and intentions which are equally potent; and the recent interest in considering the environment as a communicating system,[3] as a tissue of signs and symbols, will also have its impact. As already mentioned, it makes more sense to say that in so far as men are controlled, it is by the totality of signs in their culture and not by their economic relations alone. Thus the theory of signs, semiology, takes on a fundamental importance because it treats all the various communicating systems, from cinema to clothing to architecture, as forming understandable areas of signification.

(103) **Alison** and **Peter Smithson** *House of the Future* 1956: this plastic house goes beyond other futurist projects in adopting a principle from the automobile industry: every panel is different in each house but repeated in the next. With automation all panels could be different in each and every house, as in the past. In the foreground the living room is seen with raisable table, service trolley and other gadgets; behind this are the patio, bathroom and dressing area.

1 Robert Venturi,
*Complexity and Contradiction
in Architecture,* Museum of
Modern Art, New York,
1966

Without going into the theory of semiology in any depth, one can say that one of its contributions will be to clarify the relations between the variety of collective resources, the *langue,* and the individual's selection and creation from this, the *parole.* The architect will be increasingly using signs from heterogeneous sources, including actual signboards themselves (104), in order to communicate with a pluralistic and fragmented society. The problem of using clichés, which will be manufactured at an increasing rate, without being either condescending or trivial will depend on the architect's reading of the *langue.* If he uses resources which are too distant from collective expectation, he will fail to communicate, whereas if he does not change the context of a cliché, he will erode the *langue* and also fail to communicate, the message remaining below the threshold of consciousness. Robert Venturi has shown and explained[1] how the architect can incorporate clichés, images and advertisement into a building without falling into either of these two extremes. He does so mostly by changing the context of the cliché so that it either contrasts with the other forms or ambiguously spills over from one surface to another (105). 'Contradiction and ambiguity' are two ways of ordering diverse experience rather than suppressing it, as Fascist architecture does, behind a monolithic, integrated façade. Obviously in a pluralist society the obligation is to recognize the variety of conflicting claims and articulate the social realm for every different person in every different social situation, two jobs which Venturi fulfills by incorporating contradictory material without compromising one part with another. The vulgar remains undebased and the serious formally convincing. The two confront each other unequivocally. Another way of incorporating pluralistic meaning is through its literal articulation: instead of packaging various functions behind a blank surface, one signifies their existence by a change in material, texture or colour.

(104) **Robert Venturi**
Bill-Ding-Board a Football
Hall of Fame, 1968: the
huge two-dimensional billboard which flashes out
scores and images contrasts
with the three-dimensional
museum behind which also
acts as a grandstand. The
incorporation of diverse
meaning into architecture
will become more necessary
in an information rich
society.

(105) **Robert Venturi**
Interior of the *museum*:
on the ceiling, like the
barrel vault of a
Romanesque church, are
projected images of the
current heroes and the
reason for their elevation
to the position of sainthood.
The ambiguity between
solid and void, surface and
image, is created
intentionally by projecting
slides and movies over
various objects.

The architect José Luis Sert has followed Le Corbusier's lead in this direction, extending his approach to a wider variety of forms and materials (106, 107). In his Boston University

(106a) **José Luis Sert** and Associates, *Boston University Complex*, 1965-8: on either side of the classroom tower are two libraries and, extreme right, the student union building. The scale of this large complex is made comprehensible by breaking up the large volumes and articulating the surface, edges and units of construction.

Complex, Sert breaks down a gigantic volume into several related forms and spaces which announce the differences in function. These differences are further articulated by using separate materials, and by making the construction apparent. All this rich articulation has the effect of explaining a diverse and possibly overwhelming complexity without falling into strident rhetoric or eroded symbolism. It shows the possible discourse men can have with their environment when forms and functions are related through continual feedback. In fact, as semiology shows, the relations between form and function, or signifier and signified, are hardly ever deterministic and usually always a question of convention and continual, unrelenting interplay. Thus the Semiological School, in its attempt to make a complex environment significant will emphasize the appropriateness and plausibility of form within a social continuum. It will include material that the

(107) *Boston University Complex*: a proportional system divides the surface up into its basic components: classrooms, offices, auditoria, circulation space and library under the light scoops. Compare with Le Corbusier's Algiers scheme (pl. 101).

other traditions suppress and by this inclusion reconcile contending forces and admit the complexity of modern life. It is only such an inclusive architecture which can resist an ironic or witty attack and accommodate all the contradictory levels of the psyche, all the different thoughts and feelings which are normally constricted and suppressed. If the information-rich society is to become comprehensible it will be because the various minority groups which compose it will find their functions and forms recognized and made articulate.

10 The shift in belief

I don't believe in God, but I don't believe in man either. Humanism has failed. It didn't prevent the monstrous acts of our generation. It has lent itself to excusing and justifying all kinds of horrors. It has misunderstood man. It has tried to cut him off from all other manifestations of nature.
Claude Lévi-Strauss, *Time Magazine* June 30, 1967

In any book on the future, especially the future of the next thirty years, there has to be speculation on the kinds of emergent philosophies and beliefs which may arise. It may be naive to assume that we are living in a privileged time when major shifts occur in metaphysics, or what used to be called the *Weltanschauung*, but consider how beliefs would be affected if a cybernetic machine were constructed, capable of creative thought, self-reproduction, and out-thinking man in every respect, or if, through genetic engineering, man became capable of transforming the human species into, hopefully, a superior form of creature: man's view of himself would undergo a cataclysmic mutation. While most of the experts concerned are sceptical about either event occurring before the year 2000, particularly on a large scale, they do anticipate them being possible in the twenty-first century, so that as this point in time draws nearer there is likely to be a shift in belief and philosophy which can comprehend the emergent realities. Already, it seems to me, this shift has in many respects occurred.

On the one hand, men are disposed to regard nature and culture and the machine as similar sorts of thing because they can no longer, literally, distinguish between them. A flight over any sprawling megalopolis will reveal the loss of boundary between country and city, a distinction which characterized all pre-industrial societies. But this is just one of the many examples of the merging between nature and culture which is now taking place. With modern techniques, the indoors and outdoors are merging, as are the qualities of day and night, summer and winter and north and south. Soon large portions of the population will inhabit a city-country which is air-conditioned, lit for the twenty-four hour cycle, and fully serviced and alive with activity for a continual period (4). Already parts of every megalopolis have these pockets of totally artificial environment where the 'natural' cycles have become fully obscured: any large airport terminal for instance. But consider the substitution for, and physical superiority of artificial materials over natural. When synthetic wood and stone can be manufactured which out-perform and are visually indistinguishable from their natural counterparts, then it becomes pedantic and effete to insist on having the 'real' material. Besides, what is the 'nature' of 'real' material when all materials are inter-convertible and can be changed from one to another by atomic restructuring. Indeed for that matter what is 'human nature' when it can be increasingly directed by genetic engineering? Or alternatively, what is an 'act of nature', when men have so much knowledge that they can unleash vast 'natural' forces such as those locked in the atom, which in turn set off chains of events on a cosmic scale. Could there be a point reached where men

1 Of course it is a bit premature to speculate on this score as no one really knows whether the universe is an open or closed system. The latter position is held by Norbert Wiener who predicts the ultimate heat-death of the universe; see his *The Human Use of Human Beings*, Sphere Books, London, 1968, pp. 28–44

2 *Ibid.*, p. 14, 33–4

3 See I. A. Richards *Principles of Literary Criticism*, Routledge and Kegan Paul, London 1924 edition, p. 57

4 *Ibid.*, pp. 181, 61

could no longer measure nature or the universe without measuring themselves and implicating their instruments? At this theoretical limit, which is already reached in sub-atomic physics, there would be no further endogenous laws: all nature would be implicated with the culture that was trying to comprehend it.

The visual blurring of the difference between nature and culture in the environment, is paralleled by the reconceptualization of nature and culture effected by the increase in man's knowledge and development. Once we recognize *natural* life as carrying on a kind of *cultural* discourse with itself through the language of genetics, composing new sentences, trying out hypothetical questions as it were, then our understanding of both has shifted as we regard each as a certain level of organized system. The machine has also undergone a similar radical, conceptual, change. Formerly regarded positively by some as 'just a tool' and negatively by such critics as William Blake, Mumford and Marcuse as a degrading, monotonous weapon that reduces men to its low-level requirements, it has now reached the point of development where, in some respects, it can be more sensitive, precise, rational and perhaps even 'human' than men. Hence Andy Warhol's ironic plea 'I want to be a machine' may be made quite seriously in the future. In general systems theory the machine, nature and culture are all just different levels of organized system working in opposition to the trend towards entropy or disorganization. This opposition may emerge as the most fundamental polarity underlying man's belief and experience. The general trend of matter toward its most dispersed, disorganized state – the ultimate quiescence, monotony and randomness which the Second Law of Thermodynamics postulates as the outcome of the universe[1] – is countered by the tendency for the three 'privileged' systems to increase in their order and complexity. One might imagine a morality based on this distinction which identified the good with those systems which are continually self-transcendent and the bad with those that become more and more simple, monotonous and disorganised.[2] Thus the nature/culture/

machine distinction would be replaced by the more organized/less organized distinction and complexity would, *ipso facto*, be better than simplicity.

Such ideas in a specific sense are not new and have been in currency at least since Herbert Spencer popularized and, in a sense, also neutralized them through his one-sided over-emphasis at the end of the nineteenth century. In a general sense, one might say they are assumed by every advocate of civilization who argues that the effect of one good mind on another is beneficient or that 'the best that is thought and felt' is transferable through literature, architecture or any social discourse and will increase the organized perceptions of those who experience them. In a crude sense, the theory of culture and education which has always been practiced is, as the current adage puts it, 'you are what you eat'. In our century, no one has pursued this theory of culture, albeit in different terms, further than the literary critic I. A. Richards. He justifies the reading of literature or the experiencing of any artifact that is highly organized for its effect on ordering our psychic life and preparing its future organization. Thus,

'We pass as a rule from a chaotic to a better organized state by ways which we know nothing about. Typically through the influence of other minds. Literature and the arts are the chief means by which these influences are diffused.'[3]

The arts induce this state of organization in us more effectively than the sciences because the artist is capable of presenting and reconciling a wide range of impulses whereas the scientist or statesman can concentrate at best on a few.

'[The artist is most distinguished from the ordinary person] in the range, delicacy and freedom of the connections he is able to make between different elements of his experience. . . . His experiences . . . represent conciliation of impulses which in most minds are still confused, intertrammelled and conflicting. His work is the ordering of what in most minds is disordered.'[4]

And this state of complex ordering is transferred through a work of art, ultimately transforming the viewer so that he too can attain a balance of conflicting impulses, an inclusive view that is truly disinterested, that reconciles the usually suppressed, deranged or conflicting faculties of the psyche.

These ideas of increasing order and complexity are therefore not new to either the theory of civilization or the idea of cultural value and its transmission. They are to be found in general systems theory, the evolutionist philosophy of Ludwig von Bertalanffy and the theory of technological development of Buckminster Fuller. As far as they go, they seem to me correct and point the way to understanding basic issues of the future. Yet, as Lévi-Strauss shows, they can lead to some disastrous over-simplifications and tragic social consequences. On the one hand, complexity and technological development are often mistaken for mental superiority.[1] Every technically advanced civilization tends to consider its less-developed neighbour incapable of its scientific thought or rigorous distinctions, whereas in fact the mental capacity and scientific method of the two are equally exacting and acute. The difference is not in the kind or quality of thought, but rather in the degree to which it has been systematized and extended from its initial base as a storehouse of concepts. But the fact that many people regard this difference in degree as a difference in kind leads to all types of cultural imperialism, from ethnocentric racialism to the more subtle forms of ideology justifying meritocracy.

On the other hand, the danger of regarding superior organization in men as the purpose of civilization, as I. A. Richards and many others do, is the same as that of humanism and pragmatism. When men, or even their superior organized nervous systems, become 'the measure of all things', then truth becomes relativized beyond control and men become victims of other men and themselves. Without a court of appeal outside of man, that transcends man, that is true or false regardless of what men hold; all thought and action will be corrupted by power. All disputes between men will tend to be resolved by the strongest and this will lead to 'the

1 See Claude Lévi-Strauss, *The Savage Mind*, Weidenfeld and Nicolson, London 1968

1 See Karl Popper
Conjectures and Refutations
Routledge and Kegan Paul,
London, 1961, especially
the chapter on 'Three
Views Concerning Human
Knowledge'

2 See pages 29–32, 51, 68,
97

3 The argument is hardly
new and it has as yet not
been accepted by most
evolutionists. For an
exposition of this argument
see L. L. Whyte, *Internal
Factors in Evolution*,
Tavistock Publications,
London 1965 and Arthur
Koestler, *The Ghost in the
Machine, op. cit.* particularly
chapter 10

monstrous acts' of which Lévi-Strauss speaks, which are continually perpetrated by dictatorships and pragmatists alike. We have already seen (p. 20ff) how pragmatism and fatalism join hands to justify any sort of compromise and the reason is simply that man is taken to be the measure of truth. Almost all of the classic religions were well aware of this problem and continually acted as alternatives to temporal power and such utterly debased philosophies as 'might makes right', 'all truth is relative' and 'God is on the side of strong armies'. The greatest problem today is that with 'the disappearance of God', or a regulative idea of truth which transcends men, there is little check on temporal power and relativism. All truth becomes a matter of opinion and is manipulated by one group or another for its limited and provincial ends.

Yet it seems that these ideas of pragmatism and humanism are now reaching such a stage of bankruptcy because of their unfortunate consequences and philosophical dubiety, that the beliefs of the future may well return to the idea of transcendental truth if only to avoid these pitfalls. The philosopher Karl Popper has developed just such a concept of truth.[1] On the one hand, it shares with pragmatism the idea that truth is never *known* with certainty and on the other hand it shares with absolutism the idea that absolute truth certainly *exists*. It is approached, but never reached, through the dual aspect of conjecture and refutation, or hypothesis and testing. This duality reflects the physical situation that it is always a person who is speculating on things external to himself. The only way he can reduce error and approach truth is through constant and vigilant criticism of ideas or models of reality in himself. Yet these ideas always refer to things which transcend him and will continue to be either true or false, possible or impossible, factual or bogus irrespective of what he believes or desires.

Popper calls this method of approaching truth 'critical rationalism' to underline the fact that it needs both rational thought *and* criticism to work in a synergetic way. Either one alone would fail. For the same reason, I have used the dualistic concept 'critical evolution' (p. 32) to recognize the fact that natural evolution, from a human point of view, is not enough and that criticism of its alternatives is needed. As has been pointed out, the idea of critical evolution is opposed to the idea of determinism, because the former assumes that it is possible for men to direct their own course of development if they dissect the 'natural', wholistic systems, suppress the negative consequences and recombine the positive ones into a new system. The concept of dissectibility has been a constant *leitmotif* of this book[2] and its importance for critical evolution is that the positive aspects of different systems can always be combined if enough energy and skill are expended. We can combine semi-autonomous systems to direct our evolution in a variety of ways: through piecemeal shopping, through *ad hoc* legislative reform, through political action and even through transplant surgery and genetic engineering.

That natural evolution also works with ready-made sub-systems and their recombination is also argued here. Instead of an *external* natural selection operating on the random mutations caused by chance and cosmic radiation as the neo-Darwinians contend – it is argued that it proceeds *mostly* by *internal* selection within the organism, operating with homeostatic feedback and self regulation. That is, it is now becoming evident that genetic mutations must be selected on a molecular, chromosomal and cellular level even before they get outside, in the form of an individual, to be selected by the environment.[3] Thus evolution is not merely random, nor even largely a result of natural selection, unless one calls 'nature' by the term 'culture' and places it within the genetic subsystems of animals. The internal factors consist of the mutual interactions of all the sub-systems with the whole, a condition that is called individual homeostasis. Thus, for instance, if a mutant gene for the retina of the eye occurs by accident or chance, it will have to satisfy all the other selective pressures of the related sub-systems: the iris, the lens, the pupil, the cornea, and the size of the eye, in order to survive.

'Several people have shown that if, by some

(108) *Animal-headed people* were popular in the Middle Ages for illustrating moral fables. From woodcuts in *Monstrorum Historia* by Ulisse Aldrovandi, 1642.

experimental means, the retina and eyeball are made larger than usual, that in itself will cause a larger lens to appear, of at least approximately the appropriate size for vision. There is no reason, therefore, why a chance mutation should not affect the whole organ in a harmonious way; and there is a reasonable possibility that it might improve it. . . . A random change in a hereditary factor will, in fact, not usually result in an alteration in just one element of the adult animal: it will bring about a shift in the whole developmental system, and may thus alter the complex organ as a whole.'[1]

If this homeostatic principle operates in individual development (ontogeny) and if, as D'Arcy Thompson shows, it operates in species development (phylogeny), then we are led directly to question the possible courses of evolution and their possible limitation. Ever since the ancient Egyptians at least, men have been speculating on the possible combinations of several sorts of animal with man to create a chimera, a centaur or mermaid. In fact, the *homo*

monstrosus (108) is not a recent creation of science fiction or biological surgery but appears to be a constant speculation of men. Can these chimeras really be created; do they in fact already exist on another planet? No doubt with transplant surgery and immuno-suppressive drugs, one can construct hybrid monsters which will live for a while. Indeed, the Russians created a dog with two heads in 1963 and the Americans have kept a monkey's brain alive for several hours *in vitro.*, and there appears to be no theoretical reason why other multiple combinations could not be physically successful. But why, apart from ghoulish reasons, would anyone wish to create these hybrids? Biologists give several reasons.[2] They could fuse several animals into one, new superbreed so that it could operate in specialized environments with, say, a giraffe's legs and an ant-eater's dexterous snout. Or, they could induce human organs from the tissue of a baby and grow them on other animals so that if the donor has an accident or loses an organ, they could be retransplanted with no fear of tissue rejection. If we apply an analogous argument

1 C. H. Waddington, quoted from Koestler, *ibid*, p. 131

2 See G. R. Taylor, *op. cit.*, pp. 78–82

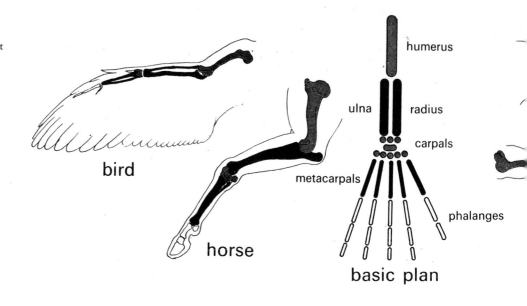

bird

horse

humerus

ulna
radius

carpals

metacarpals

phalanges

basic plan

1 Denis Diderot, *Rameau's Nephew and D'Alembert's Dream*, translated by L. W. Tancock, Penguin Books, London, 1966, p. 173

2 See G. R. Taylor, *ibid*, p. 205

to genetic engineering, we can see other advantages which have long been pointed out and desired. One could create from the start those genetic mixtures which lead to certain qualities. As Diderot prophesied in his *Dream of D'Alembert*,[1] the future genetic expert might work in 'a warm room, lined with little phials, each one bearing a label: warriors, magistrates, philosophers, poets, bottles for courtiers, bottles for prostitutes, bottles for kings'. The desired bottles could be mixed and, in so far as genetics determine personality, the particular character-types be created. Gordon Rattray Taylor foresees the creation of man-animal chimeras and organ regeneration by the year 2000 while real genetic engineering, as opposed to this bottled variety, may take place some time after this.[2] These predictions are the common stock of biological experts and are made as a

matter of course, as a routine extrapolation. As the revolutionists of May said 'TOUT EST POSSIBLE', man is infinitely plastic and anything can be done to change him. Or can it?

What if there is at work some evolutionary limitation which would act like the principle of indeterminacy in nuclear physics? Suppose that every time one tried to change a gene for a positive characteristic, it led to a chain of unforeseen and unforeseeable consequences. Or suppose there were some evolutionary mechanism, akin to individual homeostasis, that only allowed certain genetic mutations to pass through and not others. This mechanism would act like an evolutionary universal, an homologous structure (109), that limited the possible routes open to the future. Its existence would compare with that of the Platonic realm of ideal

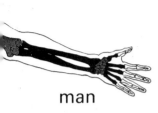

man

reptile

archetypes, or the Corbusian concept of *'objet-types'* (page 112) which were absolute and forever only possible. Except that unlike archetypes, this mechanism would not be a single, fixed entity, but be composed of multiple, flexible models which allowed a restricted range of alternatives. The existence of these models would entail that there are only certain possible ways for evolution to procede, or in other words, that there are only limited ways of being a man, or any kind of animal. If this were true, not only would the chimeras and bug-eyed monsters of science fiction be impossible in the long run, but any other extra-terrestial life, which may soon be discovered, would turn out to resemble our own in its broad outlines. Is it a coincidence that the design of telechiric devices as they become more sophisticated, resemble the homologous structures which

are found in vertebrates? Are there just a few ways of being a climbing animal that can negotiate a rough terrain? (91). What of the linguistic universals that Noam Chomsky postulates underlie all natural languages, some of which have to be built into any information-processing automata; or the structural universals which Lévi-Strauss contends can be found in every society?[1]

It would appear that the discoveries which we will see on these fronts will lead to new forms of belief which have a curious resemblance to the old in several respects. First of all, they will hold that certain transcendental truths do in fact exist outside men, which limit his possible development, as well as that of the natural species in general. Secondly, these truths will never be known with certainty, but will be assumed to exist and will be approached through a constant dialectic between hypothesis and testing. Thirdly, they will act as a general limitation on a very abstract, formal level, rather than, for instance, a level of innate ideas or particular forms which are fixed for all time. And lastly, while always existing as an absolute possibility, they will come into being in time, just as the possible forms of mathematics have always potentially existed and yet have had to be discovered and invented in history. The curious point about evolution is that everything is not possible and that the large variety of things which are, come into being at a certain moment in time as if that which is eternally possible could only be actualized by the transient. Why these eternal possibles, rather than others, should underlie every actual thing is a matter for endless speculation and primitive wonder.

1   Noam Chomsky, *Syntactic Structures,* Mouton, The Hague, 1957; *Psycholinguistics,* edited by Charles Osgood & Thomas A. Sebeok, Indiana University Press, 1965, expecially the article by George Miller, 'The Psycholinguists', pp. 293–307. For Lévi-Strauss see *Structural Anthropology,* Basic Books Inc. New York, 1963, pp. 31–55, 206–231, 277–345; and George Steiner, 'Conversation with Lévi-Strauss', *Encounter,* April 1966, p. 37. The argument for cultural universals has been put by Robin Fox in 'The Cultural Animal', *Encounter,* July 1970, pp. 31–42

Bibliography

Bibliography

General and Philosophical

Arendt, Hannah *The Human Condition* University of Chicago Press, Chicago, 1958
'Reflections on Violence' *New York Review of Books* New York, 27 February, 1969

Barthes, Roland *Elements of Semiology* Jonathan Cape, London, 1967; Hill and Wang, New York, 1968

Chomsky, Noam *American Power and the New Mandarins* Pantheon Books, New York, 1969; Penguin Books, Harmondsworth, England, 1969
Syntactic Structures Mouton, The Hague, 1957; Humanistic Press, New York, 1959

Cockburn, Alexander and Robin Blackburn, eds. *Student Power* Penguin Books, Harmondsworth, England, 1969

Cohn-Bendit, Daniel and Gabriel *Obsolete Communism The Left Wing Alternative* Andre Deutsch, London, 1968

Ellul, Jacques *The Technological Society* Jonathan Cape, London, 1965; Knopf, New York, 1964

Emery, F. E., ed. *Systems Thinking* Penguin Books, Harmondsworth, England, 1969

Huxley, Julian *Evolution in Action* Penguin Books, Harmondsworth, England, 1963; Harper and Row, New York, 1953

Koestler, Arthur *The Ghost in the Machine* Hutchinson and Co., London, 1967; Macmillan Co., New York, 1968

Lévi-Strauss, Claude *Structural Anthropology* Basic Books, London and New York, 1963
The Savage Mind Weidenfeld and Nicolson, London, 1966; University of Chicago Press, Chicago, 1967
The Scope of Anthropology Jonathan Cape, London, 1967; Humanities Press, New York, 1968

Marek, Kurt *Yestermorrow: Notes on Man's Progress* Andre Deutsch, London, 1961; Alfred A. Knopf, New York, 1961

McLuhan, H. Marshall *Understanding Media: the Extensions of Man* Routledge and Kegan Paul, London, 1964; McGraw, Toronto, 1964

Mumford, Lewis *The Story of Utopias* Viking Press, New York, 1922

Platt, John Rader *The Step to Man* Wiley, London and New York, 1966

Popper, Karl R. *Conjectures and Refutations*, Routledge and Kegan Paul, London, 1963; Basic Books, New York, 1963
The Poverty of Historicism Routledge and Kegan Paul, London, 1957; Basic Books, New York, 1966

Richards, I. A. *Principles of Literary Criticism* Routledge and Kegan Paul, London, 1924; Harcourt Bruce and World, New York, 1968

Taylor, Gordon Rattray *The Biological Time Bomb* Thames and Hudson, *London*, 1968

Whyte, L. L. *Internal Factors in Evolution* Tavistock Publications Ltd, London, 1965; George Braziller, New York, 1965

Wiener, Norbert *The Human Use of Human Beings* Houghton Mifflin Company, New York, 1950

Young, Michael *The Rise of the Meritocracy* Thames and Hudson, London, 1958

Architecture and the Future

Alexander, Christopher *Notes on the Synthesis of Form*, Oxford University Press, 1964; Harvard University Press, Cambridge, 1964
'A City is not a Tree', *Design*, London, February 1966

Anderson, Stanford, ed. *Planning for Diversity and Choice* MIT Press, Cambridge, 1968

Buchanan, Colin *Traffic in Towns* H.M. Stationary Office, London, 1963

Choay, Françoise *L'Urbanisme, Utopies et Réalitiés* Editions du Seuil, Paris, 1965

Cook, Peter *Archigram* 1–9 London, 1969
Architecture: Action and Plan Studio Vista, London, 1967; Reinhold, New York, 1967
Experimental Architecture Studio Vista,

124

London, 1970; Universe Books, New York, 1970

Davidoff, Paul 'Advocacy and Pluralism in Planning' *Journal of the American Institute of Planners* Vol. I, No. 4, November, 1965

Doxiadis, C. A. *Architecture in Transition* Hutchinson and Co., London, 1963; Oxford University Press, New York, 1968

Fuller, Buckminster and **John McHale,** eds. *World Resources Inventory. World Design Science Decade* 1965–75 Southern Illinois University, Carbondale, Ill., 1963–70
Operating Manual for the Spaceship Earth Southern Illinois University Press, 1969

Goodman, Paul and **Percival** *Communitas* 2nd ed. revised, Vintage Books, New York, 1960

Gottmann, Jean *Megalopolis* The Twentieth Century Fund, New York, 1961

Jacobs, Jane *The Death and Life of Great American Cities* Penguin Books, Harmondsworth, England, 1964; Random House, New York, 1961

McHale, John '2000 +' *Architectural Design* London, February, 1967

Norberg–Schulz, Christian *Intentions in Architecture* Allen and Unwin, London, 1964; MIT Press, Cambridge, Mass.

'Pneu world' *Architectural Design* London, June, 1968

Ragon, Michel *Ou Vivrons Nous Demain?* Robert Laffont, Paris, 1963
Les Cités de l'Avenir Editions Planète, Paris, 1965
La Cité de L'An 2000 Casterman, Tournai, 1968

Richards, Brian *New Movement in Cities* Studio Vista, London, 1966; Reinhold, New York, 1966

Venturi, Robert *Complexity and Contradiction in Architecture* Museum of Modern Art, New York, 1966; W. H. Allen, London, 1968

Predictions and Methods of Forecasting

Amis, Kingsley *New Maps of Hell, A Survey of Science Fiction,* Victor Gollancz, London, 1960; Harcourt, Brace and World, New York, 1960

Armytage, W. H. G. *Yesterday's Tomorrows,* Routledge and Kegan Paul, London, 1968

Asimov, Isaac *The Caves of Steel* T. V. Boardman and Co., London, 1954; Doubleday, New York, 1954

Bell, Daniel *Toward the Year* 2000: *Work in Progress* Daedalus, Academy of Arts and Sciences, Boston, Summer 1967
'Twelve Modes of Prediction – A Preliminary Sorting of Approaches in the Social Sciences', Daedalus, Summer 1964, pp. 845–880
'Notes on the Post-Industrial Society', *The Public Interest* No. 6, 1967

Brzezinski, Z. 'America in the Technotronic Age', *Encounter,* January, 1968

Calder, Nigel, ed. *The World in 1984* 2 vols. Penguin Books, Harmondsworth, England, 1965

Clarke, Arthur C. *Profiles of the Future* Victor Gollancz, London, 1962; Harper and Row, New York, 1963

Direction de la Documentation *Réflexions pour 1985.* collection
'Documents pour le plan', Direction de la Documentation, Paris, 1964

Gabor, Dennis *Inventing the Future* Secker and Warburg, London, 1963; Alfred A. Knopf, New York, 1964

Jouvenel, Bertrand de, ed. *Futuribles: Studies in Conjecture* Vol. I, Droz, Geneva, 1963; *The Art of Conjecture* Basic Books, London and New York, 1967 and 1966

Jungk, Robert and **Johan Galtung,** eds, *Mankind* 2000 Allen and Unwin, London, 1969; Universitets Forlaget, 1969

Kahn, Herman and **Anthony J. Wiener** *Year* 2000 Macmillan and Co., London, 1967

McHale, John, *The Future of the Future* Braziller, New York, 1969

Science Journal *Forecasting the Future* London, October 1967.
Machines Like Men October 1968

Young, Michael, ed. *Forecasting and the Social Sciences* Heinemann, London, 1968

Banham, Reyner 'The Great Gizmo' *Industrial Design* September, 1965

Eco, Umberto and **G. B. Zorzoli** *A Pictorial History of Inventions* Weidenfeld and Nicolson, London, 1962; Macmillan Co., New York, 1963

Giedion, Sigfried *Mechanisation Takes Command* Oxford University Press, Oxford and New York, 1948

Ginzberg, Eli, ed. *Technology and Social Change* Columbia University Press, New York, 1964

Jewkes, J. et al. *The Sources of Invention* Macmillan and Co., London, 1958; St Martin's Press, New York, 1958

Koestler, Arthur *The Act of Creation* Hutchinson, London, 1964; Macmillan and Co., New York, 1964

Kubler, George *The Shape of Time* Yale University Press, New Haven, 1962

Mazlish, Bruce, ed. *The Railroad and the Space Program: An Exploration in Historical Analagy* MIT Press, Cambridge, Mass., 1966

Morison, Eltin *Men, Machines, and Modern Times* MIT Press, Cambridge, Mass., 1966

Photo-acknowledgements

Publisher and author would like to thank the following for their permission to use photographs in this book: Agip 68; Air India, London 5; Alexander, Christopher 95; American Embassy 74; Archigram 80-84, 93; Avincola, Rome 85, 86; Baer, Morley, California 33; Banham, Reyner 44; Bauhaus-Archiv, Darmstadt 22; Bayer, Kenneth 20; B.B.C. 109; Bell Aerosystems, New York 15a, 16; Bouldadon, Gabriel, Institute, Geneva 53, 55; Brazilian Embassy, London 2, 3; Cardot Véra 51; Council of Industrial Design, London 103; Cousteau, Jean-Michel 88; Crompton, Dennis 94b; Dallegret, François 44; Debord, Guy 69; Dawns, Surrey 36; Eames, Charles, California 45a, 45b; Einzix, Richard 100 b. c. d; Electricity Council, London 52b; Energy Conversion Ltd 42; Eurda, Paris 50; Ford Motor Company 52c, 54; Friedman, Yona 46, 47; Futagawa, Y. Tokyo 18b, 18c; General Electric, New York 90, 91; Good Year 57; Graph-Lit, Paris 17; Grassi, Siena 31; Guérin, Johnstone, Goge Inc., California 43a, 43b; Hervé, Lucien, Paris 101; Hervochon, Yves, Paris 1; Hollein, Hans 76, 77; Holm, Stig, Stockholm 39a; Homelex 34; Ishimoto Architectural, Tokyo 18a; Jencks, Charles 25, 28, 30, 37, 40, 100a; Joly, Pierre 51; Jungmann, J.P. 72, 73; Kawasumi, Tokyo 59, 60; Kahn, Hermann 58; Ku-Khanh, Paris 52a; Library of Congress, Kent Grimm 10; Lockhead Missiles and Space Company, California 96-9; Lousada, Sandra, London 56; Mangin, William 63, 65; Magnum 67; Moderna Museet, Stockholm 6; Nowca, Dusseldorf 94a; Osamu Murai, Tokyo 26, 62; Phokion Karas 106a, 107; Playboy Enterprises 23; Pohl, George, Pennyslvania 104, 105; Price, Cedric 71 a, b.; Retoria, Tokyo 18 b, c; Reynolds, Submarine 89a, b; Richards, Brian, London 56; Robert, Karl, Taunus 21; Rolls Royce Limited 15b; Schaeven, Deidi von, Berlin 78a, b; *Science Journal* 14, 27; Sert, Jackson, Massachusetts 106, 107; Silver, Nathan 35; Skyphotos 41; Smithson 70; Soleri, Paolo 87; Sternbergs Bilder, Stockholm 39a; Stirling, James 66; *Times, The* 38; Turner, John 64; Unimate 102; United States Information Service 4a, 11, 12, 32, 39b, 48, 92; United States Travel Service, London 7, 8, 46; Weeks, John 29a, 29b; Wilford, Michael 9; Windenberger, Jacques, Aix-en-Provence 49; and Zanotta, Milan 75.

Index

DATE DUE

~~FEB 26 75~~			
OCT 2 78	1979		
DEC 2 1			
APR 7 1983			
DEC 9 1984			
DEC 0 7 2006			
GAYLORD			PRINTED IN U.S.A.